ISIDORE OF SEVILLE

De Ecclesiasticis Officiis

Ancient
Christian
Writers

THE WORKS OF THE FATHERS IN TRANSLATION

MANAGING EDITOR
Dennis D. McManus

EDITORIAL BOARD
John Dillon

No. 61

ISIDORE OF SEVILLE:
DE ECCLESIASTICIS OFFICIIS

TRANSLATION AND INTRODUCTION

BY

REV. THOMAS L. KNOEBEL, PhD

THE NEWMAN PRESS
New York/Mahwah, N.J.

Jacket design by Cynthia Dunne

Library of Congress Cataloging-in-Publication Data

Isidore, of Seville, Saint, d. 636.
    [De ecclesiasticis officiis. English]
    Isidore of Seville : De ecclesiasticis officiis / translation and introduction by Thomas L. Knoebel.
        p. cm. — (Ancient Christian writers ; no. 61)
    Includes bibliographical references and index.
    ISBN-13: 978-0-8091-0581-6 (alk. paper)
    1. Catholic Church—Liturgy. 2. Catholic Church—Clergy. I. Knoebel, Thomas L. (Thomas Louis), 1943– II. Title.
    BR65.I73D4313 2008
    264´.0200946—dc22

                                      2007051139

Published by The Newman Press
an imprint of Paulist Press
997 Macarthur Boulevard
Mahwah, New Jersey 07430

www.paulistpress.com

PRINTED AND BOUND IN THE UNITED STATES OF AMERICA

CONTENTS

v

PREFACE

Over thirty years ago, as a young priest doing doctoral studies, I happened to visit Toledo in Spain. I found my way into the cathedral and discovered the chapel in which the Mozarabic Rite Mass was still being celebrated on a daily basis. I was captivated by the rite and what I knew of its history. The memory of this visit never left me.

Many years later, through a series of fortuitous events, I found myself back in this same chapel, this time as an academic dean of a seminary, one of whose faculty members was doing his own doctoral work on the Good Friday liturgy in the Mozarabic Rite. I grew to know more about the rite and became acquainted with its present-day chaplains. They invited me to concelebrate Eucharist and pray Lauds with them in the rite on a daily basis during my visits. Eventually, on June 18, 2000, the cardinal archbishop of Toledo invested me as an honorary member of *La Ilustre y Antiquísima Hermandad de Caballeros Mozárabes de Nuestra Señora de la Esperanza de la Imperial Ciudad de Toledo (Hermandad Mozárabe)*. The Hermandad is the official organization of families descended by blood from the original Mozarabic community living in Spain.

This entire spiritual pilgrimage led me to discover the crucially important role played by Isidore of Seville (d. 636) in the development of the Mozarabic Rite. To help make his contribution better known, I propose to provide the first complete English translation of *De Ecclesiasticis Officiis* (DEO), his major work in this regard. Although bits and pieces of DEO have been translated by others, who cite it for their own purposes, to date no translation of this important work by a leading figure of the Spanish church has appeared in any modern language, including Spanish, French, and German. A new, critical Latin text was published in 1989, edited by Christopher M. Lawson, in Corpus Christianorum, Series Latina 113. I am using this critical edition for my translation.

In its present form, DEO consists of two books with a total of seventy chapters. Book 1 is organized on the basis of the liturgical practice of Isidore's day and describes the eucharistic liturgy with its

vii

components, the Divine Office, and major liturgical feasts and church practices. The fact that these chapters are arranged in the order of Spain's seventh-century liturgy provides modern-day scholars and interested Catholics with a fascinating glimpse into a vibrant liturgical prayer form that continues to be celebrated today, some fifteen hundred years later. It is this rite that nourished the faith of the Christian community in Spain, struggling to survive through the seven hundred years Spain was occupied and governed by the Islamic peoples who spread into the peninsula from northern Africa. In honor of the major role this liturgical rite played in the survival of Christianity through these many centuries, the rite was allowed to survive and be celebrated as one of only two non-Roman Latin liturgical rites in the West.

In book 2 of DEO, Isidore studies the offices of those who exercised ministry in the church of that day, describes other significant groups, and concludes by examining the Rite of Initiation. Book 2 provides a rare account of church life and practice of that era.

My research in Spain over the past several years confirms that DEO served as a foundational document for the recent renewal of the Hispano-Mozarabic Rite in Spain and for the publication in 1991 of new liturgical books for the rite. Interviews with members of the commission entrusted with this work, including its secretary Don Cleofé Sánchez Montealegre, have indicated its importance for their work. DEO provides foundational sources for the structure of the Spanish eucharistic liturgy in the seventh century. It also represents the first liturgical sourcebook in the West after the period of *libelli*.

In addition to his liturgical role, St. Isidore, Doctor of the Church, had great influence in the development of Catholic doctrine and practice. He is widely renowned as a leading figure of the Spanish church and is credited as being the intellectual and spiritual force behind the flourishing of the Spanish church in the seventh century. His works were copied prolifically throughout the medieval period. For many medieval historians, including Jocelyn Hillgarth and Yves Congar, the influence of Isidore was immense, reaching to the time of the Reformation.

Throughout the previous century, there have been periodic renewals of interest in Isidorian studies. For example, on the occasion of the thirteenth centenary of his death and the fourteenth of his birth, major works have appeared: La Provincia de Andalucía S.J., ed.,

Miscellanea Isidoriana: Homenaje a S. Isidoro de Sevilla en el XIII Centenario de su Muerte 636—4 de Abril—1936 (Rome: Gregorian University Press, 1936) and Manuel C. Díaz y Díaz, ed., *Isidoriana: Estudios sobre San Isidoro de Sevilla en el XIV Centenario de su nacimiento* (León, Spain: Centro de Estudios "San Isidoro," 1961).

Isidore's better-known work, the *Etymologies,* is the only work of his that has been translated into English to date. It has recently been the subject of much discussion in some scholarly circles, particularly as people speculate about Isidore's designation as the patron saint of the Internet. See, for example, Rachel L. Stocking, *Bishops, Councils, and Consensus in the Visigothic Kingdom, 589–633* (Ann Arbor: University of Michigan Press, 2000).

Moreover, the renewed interest in sacramental theology occasioned by the liturgical renewal and current scholarly work on the theological notion of inculturation will provide an audience for this translation. Furthermore, those interested in medieval history and religion will find in this work a window into the life and practices of an influential segment of the Western church. In addition, those interested in exploring the spiritual, liturgical, and religious roots of the growing U.S. Hispanic population will find in this document worthwhile research material.

I would like to conclude by acknowledging the tremendous assistance rendered by Dr. Nancy de Flon, my editor at Paulist Press. In addition, I am indebted to Rev. Raúl-Gómez, SDS, PhD, a colleague at Sacred Heart School of Theology, for collaborating with me in the writing of the introduction to this work. Rev. Gómez is an expert in the Hispano-Mozarabic Rite. I also want to express my deep gratitude to the members of the Hermandad Mozárabe, especially D. Mario Arellano García and the parishioners of the Mozarabic rite parish of Santa Eulàlia y San Marcos, Toledo. Also thanks to the Mozarabic rite chaplains, especially D. Enrique Carrillo Morales; to members of the commission charged with the renewal of the rite, especially D. Cleofé Sánchez Montealegre and D. Jaime Colomina Torner; and finally, to D. Ramón Gonzálvez Ruiz, former director of the Cathedral Archives and Library.

Thomas L. Knoebel

INTRODUCTION

Christopher M. Lawson has provided scholars of St. Isidore of Seville with a new critical edition of Isidore's *De Ecclesiasticis Officiis* (DEO).[1] In this present book I provide the first English translation of his critical edition, making this important text accessible to a wider audience. The critical edition was begun by Christopher Lawson's father, A. C. Lawson.[2] After extensive new research of the sources, Christopher M. Lawson completed his father's work, but died prior to seeing its publication. Jocelyn N. Hillgarth received permission to publish the work according to the terms of Lawson's will.[3] Thus, it was published posthumously as volume 113 of the Corpus Christianorum, Series Latina in 1989.

What follows is a brief introduction providing a short biography of St. Isidore of Seville, a summary of his literary output, his significance as a father and doctor of the church, and an overview of DEO.[4] I highlight and spend considerable time on the context of DEO in terms of the liturgies of the Latin West and its importance for the development and renewal of the Hispano-Mozarabic Rite. I complete the introduction with a list of the sources used by Isidore in the writing of DEO as determined by Lawson.

A SHORT BIOGRAPHY OF ST. ISIDORE

The basic facts concerning Isidore are well known and attested to in the literature on him.[5] Most sources report that Isidore was born sometime around AD 560.[6] His father, a man named Severianus, was originally from Cartagena in the southeastern part of Iberia. This city was the ancient capital of the Carthaginians in Iberia and was occupied during a considerable portion of the sixth and seventh centuries by the Byzantines. Isidore's mother, Turtur, gave birth to four children—Isidore, Leander, Fulgentius, and Florentina.[7] Leander and Fulgentius became bishops, and Florentina became an abbess; all three are revered

1

as saints. Isidore was the youngest of the four. The father's name seems to indicate a Hispano-Roman origin, while the origin of Isidore's mother is less clear. It is possible that Isidore was Hispano-Roman on his father's side and Visigothic on his mother's side.[8] At some point the family moved from Cartagena to Seville. The reasons for the move are not known, but exile resulting from the Byzantine takeover of Cartagena is the most likely cause. It is possible that Severianus, a patrician, sided with the Visigoths and thus was on the losing side. Whether Isidore was born in Cartagena or in Seville shortly after his father moved to that city—since he was born after the Byzantine takeover of Cartagena—is disputed. Roger Collins, for example, speculates that Isidore was probably born in Cartagena and is of Byzantine origin, since his name is Greek in derivation and the area was under Byzantine control.[9] The name Isidore is pagan in origin and literally means "gift of Isis." Nonetheless, the name was used by Christians as well. As an adult, Isidore was clearly in the Visigothic camp, since he viewed Gothic Hispania as the heir to the Roman Empire.[10] This fact points to the potential Visigothic origin of his mother and the Hispano-Roman origin of his father rather than to a Byzantine origin for the family.

Leander, twenty years older than Isidore, had become bishop of Seville in c. 580 and, following his father's death, became Isidore's teacher. In the episcopal school in Seville, Isidore learned the classical writings, as well as Greek. In addition, Leander formed the character of Isidore. It is not known whether Isidore became a monk, nor how he took his steps into priesthood. The first well-established date for Isidore's life is the year 600, when he was consecrated bishop of Seville, succeeding his brother Leander in the see. Records are clear that Isidore presided over the Second Council of Seville in 619 and the important Fourth Council of Toledo in 633. He governed as archbishop of Seville until his death on April 4, 636.

The years of Isidore's lifetime spanned a difficult period in Spain. After the collapse of Roman rule in the Iberian Peninsula in the early fifth century, political, religious and social life was beset by divisions until the late sixth century. Even after Alaric II (reigned 484–507) moved the seat of the Visigothic kingdom from Toulouse to Toledo in 507, large areas of the peninsula remained virtually independent. When one of the nobles appealed to the Byzantines for help in usurping the Visigoth throne, they invaded in 552 and held a portion of the southern part of the peninsula for over seventy years.

In addition, the Christian Visigoths were Arians and persecuted the Catholics in their kingdom until the Visigoths embraced orthodoxy in the 580s. Their king Reccared (reigned 586–601) converted to Catholicism in 587. Isidore had the difficult task of overcoming the remnants of Arianism in Spain, since he replaced his brother as bishop of Seville scarcely ten years after the majority of Visigoths had embraced the orthodox faith. To this end, he devoted his efforts utilizing two chief tools—the education of the clergy and the unification of liturgical practice.

In order to educate the clergy, Isidore was energetic, founding schools and insisting that each diocese have a school for the training of priests. In keeping with his scholarly vision, he made sure that all branches of knowledge, including the arts and medicine, were taught in these precursors of today's seminaries. This was the first "seminary system" in Europe. As an indication of Isidore's importance in this regard, his theological compendium, the *Sententiae*, was used for over nine hundred years—until the Council of Trent (1545–1563)—for the education of priests in Spain. Among numerous other works, he also wrote a rule for monks in an attempt to reform the monastic life.

The second of Isidore's most important accomplishments as bishop was his dedication to the unification of liturgical practices in the Visigothic realm. In this respect, *De Ecclesiasticis Officiis* (DEO; *Patrologia cursus completus: Series latina*, ed. J.-P. Migne [Paris: 1844–64], 83:737–826) is of immense importance. In it Isidore clearly describes the order of the Visigothic-era eucharistic liturgy.[11] This work becomes the major reference for later bishops and scholars largely responsible for the flourishing and preservation of this liturgy for centuries to follow, even through the long period of Muslim domination. Under the auspices of Cardinal Cisneros (1436–1517), liturgical prayers compiled for use in Seville during Isidore's time eventually formed the core of the Mozarabic missal, which was used, with some revisions, in Toledo until 1991.

Finally, as bishop of Seville for thirty-six years, Isidore set a model for representative governance in Europe. He rejected autocratic decision making and instead organized synods and provincial and general councils for the governance of the Spanish church. Most importantly, his accomplishments laid the foundation for what is known as the Carolingian renewal of church and society. This revival

marked the beginning of the Christian domination of Europe that
began in the middle of the eighth century with Charlemagne's reign.

First interred in Seville, Isidore's remains were moved to León
in 1063 at the behest of agents of Fernando I, king of Castilla y León.
Fernando desired relics of Christian martyrs, particularly the much venerated Sts. Justa and Rufina, virgins of Seville martyred under Diocletian.
Not being able to locate them, the agents requested the remains of
Isidore instead.[12] The Muslim ruler of Seville acceded to Fernando on
account of his fierce reputation, while lamenting the loss of such an illustrious figure. On December 23, 1063, Isidore's remains arrived in
León in northern Spain and were received with great pomp; they were
installed in the newly constructed basilica built in his honor. His cult
was introduced slowly into the Hispanic and European liturgical cal-
endars, and his feast day was set on April 4 by 858. In the Roman liturgical books, his feast was introduced in the sixteenth century and his
feast day was extended to the universal church. Isidore was proclaimed
a doctor of the church by Pope Innocent XIII on April 25, 1722.[13]

Summary of His Literary Output

Isidore was a major literary figure, producing at least seventeen
major works,[14] in addition to numerous letters. His last known and
most famous work, an encyclopedia of knowledge entitled the
Etymologies, was a popular textbook for nine centuries. Displaying his
classical education and his command of classical literature, Isidore also
wrote books on grammar, astronomy, geography, history, and biography as well as theology. When the Arabs brought study of Aristotle
back to Europe, this was not a novelty for Spain because Isidore's open
mind had already reintroduced the philosopher to students there.[15]

In his famous *Renotatio*, Bishop Braulio of Saragossa (bishop
631–651), a close friend of Isidore, provides a listing of Isidore's writings and offers a contemporary assessment of him:

> Isidore, an illustrious man, a bishop of the church at Seville,
> successor and brother of Bishop Leander, flourished at the
> time of Emperor Mauritius and King Reccared; in him
> antiquity gained some new fame for itself, or rather our age
> saw in him an image of antiquity, for he was a man well

trained in every kind of locution, so that the quality of his words made him adaptable for one who was learned and for one who had no knowledge, famous both for suiting his words to his subject and for his incomparable eloquence. It can now be very easy for any prudent reader to judge how great his knowledge was from his varied interests and carefully written works.[16]

It is obvious from this testimony that, even in his own time, Isidore was recognized not only as a scholar known for the breadth of his knowledge, particularly his knowledge of the wisdom of antiquity, but also as a great communicator able to speak with the most learned as well as the illiterate. That Isidore possessed rare gifts is evidenced by the wide circulation of his writings,[17] as well as their centuries-long prominence in the schools.

In this same work, Bishop Braulio provides a list of the works written by Isidore. This list has long been judged to have been arranged in chronological order, although recently some doubt has been cast on the dating of Isidore's writings.[18] Nevertheless, even though the ordering of Braulio's list has been subjected to some critique, the list retains its credibility, and the dates of Isidore's writings can be approximated. *Chronicon (Chronicles)*, the eleventh work on the list, was published in 615, and his *Regula Monastica (Monastic Rule)*, the fourteenth, was published before 618. Certain of the works, namely, *Differentiae (Differences)*, *Proemia (Introductions)*, and *De Ecclesiasticis Officiis (Offices)* (the first, second, and fourth works in Braulio's list), contain material from *Moralia in Job*, a work written in 597–598 by Pope Gregory the Great (Roman pontiff 590–604). Obviously the first books on the list cannot have been written before Gregory's work had been transmitted to Spain and read by Isidore. Thus, the great majority of Isidore's writings, including DEO, can be dated sometime between 598 and 618.[19] Those remaining, notably *Sententiae (Book of Sentences)*, were written sometime between 618 and 636, the year of Isidore's death.

Braulio's list includes comments on each of the works as seen here:[20]

He published:
1) Two books of *Differences*, in which he made subtle distinctions between the meanings of words which are commonly confused in practice.

2) One book of *Introductions*, in which he described, with brief notes, the contents of each book of Holy Scripture.

3) One book *On the Lives and Deaths of the Fathers*, in which, by means of brief sentences, he set forth the deeds, greatness, death, and burial of each.

4) Two books of *Offices* for his brother, Bishop Fulgentius, in which he revealed the origin of offices and why each one is performed in the Church of God, interpreting with his own pen, but not omitting the authority of the elders.

5) Two books of *Synonyms*, in which reason appears to exhort the soul to consolation and to the hope of obtaining pardon.

6) One book to King Sisebut *On the Nature of Things*, in which he settled some obscure points about the elements after investigating both ecclesiastical teachers and philosophers.

7) One book *On Numbers*, in which he touched, in part, upon the science of arithmetic to explain the numbers inserted in ecclesiastical writings.

8) One book *On the Names of the Law and the Gospels*, in which he explained the mystical significance of the persons mentioned.

9) One book of *Heresies*, in which he followed the examples of our elders and collected scattered topics as briefly as possible.

10) Three books of *Sentences*, adorned with choice selections from the books of Pope Gregory's Morals.

11) One book of *Chronicles* from the beginning of the world to his own time, collected with extreme brevity.

12) Two books *Against the Jews* at the request of his sister, Florentina, a nun of saintly life, in which he expressed, by quotation from the Law and the Prophets, approval of everything which the Catholic faith believes.

13) One book of *Famous Men*, to which I have added the present remarks.

14) One book of *Monastic Rule*, which he most properly tempered for use in his own country and to suit the spirits of the weak.

15) One book *On the Origin of the Goths,* and the *Kingdom of the Sueves,* and also the *History of the Vandals.*

16) Two books of *Questions,* which furnish the reader with much material from ancient commentators.

17) A manuscript of *Etymologies,* of extremely large size, set off by him by subject matter rather than in books; because he wrote it at my request, I divided it into fifteen books, although he left it unfinished. This work is suitable to every branch of philosophy; whoever reads and meditates upon it frequently will have and deserve a reputation for knowledge of both divine and human affairs. It is packed with elegant statements of many kinds, collected in concise manner; from it, there is practically nothing that cannot be learned.

There are many other smaller works of this man, as well as some well-embellished inscriptions in the church of God, for God created him in recent times to support His Church after so many disasters in Spain.

Interestingly, the eleventh book listed by Braulio, the *Chronicles,* becomes a model for a work of later Christians living in Córdoba under Muslim rule. Titled *Crónica Mozárabe,* this work, written in Latin by an anonymous author around 754, was intended to be a continuation of Isidore's opus. Like Isidore's effort, it was an attempt to chronicle historical events, but this time focused on the Mozarab community of Córdoba.[21] The title of this chronicle, *Crónica Mozárabe,* was taken up anew beginning in 1968 by the contemporary twentieth-century Mozarab community of Toledo as the title of its official publication.

ISIDORE'S SIGNIFICANCE AS ONE OF THE LATER FATHERS AND A DOCTOR OF THE CHURCH

In his book *Visigothic Spain, Byzantium, and the Irish,* J. N. Hillgarth draws on his lifelong interest in early medieval intellectual and religious history. Contrary to the "popular" opinion that seventh-century Spain under the Visigoths was the "darkest of all 'Dark'

Ages,"[22] he maintains that it played a significant role, largely through the contributions of Isidore:[23]

> Seventh-century Spain saw one of the most striking revivals of the classical tradition in the Latin West. The leading writer of the age, Isidore of Seville, was the author of perhaps the most influential book (apart from the Bible) of the whole Middle Ages, the *Etymologiae* or *Origines*. The "two faces" of Isidore, a product of Late Antiquity but a master of the Middle Ages, make him a man whose thought spans the transition between these ages.

Hillgarth maintains that an examination of Isidore's writings and of the influence they attained in subsequent centuries provides an illustration of how Visigothic Spain passed on to the rest of Europe the riches it had received from classical Antiquity and contemporary Byzantium.

Many medieval historians consider the influence of Isidore to be immense. Notable for our purposes is Yves M.-J. Congar, OP. Hillgarth notes that Congar considers Isidore to be, even more than Augustine, Jerome, Gregory, or Aristotle, "'un maître en discours logique et en définitions, un premier instituteur qui lui a enseigné l'usage raisonné de sa langue,' for he provided medieval men with 'un instrument d'ordre et, avec ses limites, de précision dans la pensée.'"[24] He further cites Congar's judgment that it is only "the Lutheran Revolution and the Dispute of Leipzig (1519), in particular, [that] marks the end of a world formed in the school of Isidore."[25]

In addition to his great learning and literary contributions, Isidore was a major figure politically. Only with the conversion of the Visigoths from Arianism to Catholicism in the 580s was a collaboration of power possible between the political and ecclesial leadership. As Rachel Stocking notes, "In 589 the Third Council of Toledo formalized the Visigoths' conversion from Arianism to Catholicism, along with the resulting alliance between *regnum* and *sacerdotium* that was meant to be the foundation for the kingdom's governance henceforth."[26]

The next half century was marked by the efforts of successive Visigothic kings and the Catholic bishops, principally Leander and Isidore, to forge a Christian kingdom of centralized rule based on political and religious unity. This included the attempt of the bishops to unify the various liturgical practices found throughout the Visigothic kingdom. Owing to the chaotic situation among the Visigothic rulers, the church under Isidore's leadership provided stability, which opened the way for the church to assert great authority over the civil leaders. One way this was done was through the quasi-sacramental practice of anointing kings.

Isidore's vision was far-reaching. Stocking assesses it in these terms:

> This vision came to be expressed in a cultural movement led by Isidore of Seville that centered on the resurrection and redefinition of Roman, Byzantine, and patristic knowledge and ideals. The cultural renewal of the seventh-century Iberian church generated an outpouring of theological and educational tracts, chronicles, saints' *Lives,* letters, poems, and liturgy.[27]

Isidore's *De Ecclesiasticis Officiis* is a major contribution to this effort.

As historians of this period of Iberian history note, Isidore became bishop of Seville after a particularly disruptive period. The church was gravely disorganized after two centuries of tribal conflicts, destruction, autonomous rule without an effective central authority, and the consequent lack of effective schooling and cultural institutions. Isidore embarked on a program of organized clerical education as a particularly effective means of reestablishing order and Christian unity in the Visigothic realms. A clergy that was well educated and morally upright would help ensure the liturgical, moral, and political stability so desired by both kings and bishops. Clerical education and discipline would support the political legislation and ecclesial synodal activity whose goal was a genuine uniformity in liturgy and morality throughout the kingdom. Isidore's work *De Ecclesiasticis Officiis* was directed toward that goal. As we will see in my translation below, the book sets out to show the origin of the most significant church instruments of order and authority. It does this by treating the liturgical and sacramental systems, as well as the offices of clerical and lay structure and order.

Undoubtedly, Isidore's efforts were embraced by the newly Catholic political rulers, for such a system of religious authority would help provide a reason for settling disputes in more amicable fashion, would lead to the establishment of order, would make the defense of the kingdom easier, and in general, would promote a more just and peaceful kingdom. Isidore's writings, liturgical legislation, and synodal activity were geared toward this project. I agree with Stocking, who concludes that Isidore and others "produced elaborate compilations of liturgy, law, and legal formulas, which together with the literary output of kings and bishops constitute a cohesive and coherent monument to their own vision of ideal Christian society and governance."[28]

This vision had its concrete beginning in 587 when the new king, Reccared (586–601), converted from Arian to Catholic Christianity in the year following his ascension to the Visigothic throne. Two years later Reccared and a group of newly converted nobles and clerics attended the Third Council of Toledo.[29] This council was the first gathering of Catholic bishops from all the Iberian provinces ever held under a Visigothic monarch. Only those bishops from the territories still held in the south by the Byzantines were absent. The king and his followers confirmed their conversion, and the Catholic bishops received their confession of the true faith with acclamations for the king. Leander, the leading bishop of the day and the presider over the council, explained in a homily that the peace achieved through the conversion of the Goths not only ended the history of suffering in the persecuted church but also served as proof that the whole world would be united within that church and thus be saved.

This opinion was shared. John of Biclar, for example, a contemporary chronicler, compared the Third Council of Toledo to the Council of Nicaea and King Reccared to Constantine. "For John, Toledo III constituted so profound a turning point in history that he linked it to the end of wars between the Byzantines and Persians and to the Persian emperor's conversion to Catholicism. The peace of the church had descended upon the entire world."[30]

Indeed, Toledo III was a significant turning point in the history of Iberia, both politically and ecclesially. As Stocking notes,

> The resounding claims of governmental, religious, and political unity made in 589 were repeated in a series of church councils held during the remaining 122 years of Visigothic rule. While the participants in Toledo called upon previous great councils of the church as models for their own actions, Toledo III itself served as a precedent for seventh-century leaders giving ceremonial expression to their governing con-

> sensus, which in time came to be equated with centralized rule over the entire peninsula from the royal city, Toledo. During the "Reconquista" the Catholic unification of the peninsula was envisioned in images derived from this Visigothic tradition. Indeed, the power of images of Visigothic unification has survived until the present in Spain: in 1989 scholars and clerics gathered in Toledo to observe the fourteenth centenary of Toledo III amid an outpouring of newspaper articles and papal messages celebrating the moment in 589 when "Spain was born."[31]

This last phrase occurs in the headline to an interview with Cardinal M. González Martín "España nació en el III Concilio de Toledo" on the occasion of the celebration of the anniversary. According to Stocking, "historians still regard Toledo III as a turning point in the Visigothic kingdom."[32]

Although this movement toward political and religious harmony began under Leander, it was his brother Isidore who carried it forward by providing the intellectual acumen and force to sustain it. This included presiding over Toledo IV in 633. He also provided the ecclesiastical stability and ongoing vision required because of his long reign and intellectual output. His writings and his consistent efforts toward clerical education, upholding moral standards, and enforcing liturgical unity produced a major force for continuity and stability. On the other hand, a series of Visigothic kings of relatively short reigns resulted in a relatively weak secular government. Beginning with Leander and Isidore, church rulers took on the role of providing stability in the midst of a chaotic secular government. The Visigothic failure to establish a strong central government over its remaining 122 years accounted, in no small part, for the ability of the Islamic invaders at the beginning of the eighth century rapidly to conquer almost all of the Iberian peninsula in the space of a year. Nonetheless, the *Reconquista*, or Reconquest, which was undertaken almost immediately by Christian warrior-rulers from the north of Spain, would look to the Visigothic *regnum* as its ideal.[33]

Isidore is accounted as the last Latin father of the church and is considered the most learned man of his time. His contemporaries proclaimed him the "oracle of Visigothic Spain, Solomon revived, savior of the Roman culture, and teacher of Europe."[34] The fathers of the Eighth

Council of Toledo declared him Doctor of Spain in 653. Already by the time of his death, his writings were spread throughout western Europe of the time by Irish and English monks. J. N. Hillgarth asserts, on the basis of textual research completed by A. C. Lawson, that it is possible to follow the diffusion of DEO via Toledo and Saragossa to Italy (ca. 640), and then from Italy to the British Isles.[35] Leading church figures throughout Europe, including St. Boniface in Germany, were ardent admirers. Isidore's renown was such that he became a luminary of the Carolingian renewal of the ninth century. Alcuin in particular used his writings to bolster his own positions in the effort to reform governance and liturgy under Charlemagne's auspices. Others did the same, including those with opposing positions. Isidore had such prestige that, with time, letters, books, formulas, and documents were attributed to him, including what had come to be known as the false decretals of Isidore based on his rules for civil and church governance, including *Hispania* and DEO. Though by the time of St. Thomas Aquinas his authority had begun to wane, Aquinas nevertheless cites Isidore's *Etymologies* to support his teachings on natural law.

Isidore was named a doctor of the church because of his writings and intellectual acumen. His writing provided the transmission of classical knowledge from antiquity and provided guidance for church and society and a source for learning that was shared throughout Christian Europe on account of its wisdom and erudition. His interpretations helped to explain the medieval world to his contemporaries. The importance of his contribution was formally recognized by the universal church in naming him a doctor of the church in 1722.

DE ECCLESIASTICIS OFFICIIS (DEO)

Listed fourth among the works Braulio attributes to Isidore, DEO was written, as stated above, between the reception of Gregory's *Moralia in Job* in Seville, which cannot be before 598, and the *Chronicon* in 615. From the very beginning there has been a lack of consensus as to the name of the work. Braulio names the book *officiorom libros duos* ("two books of offices") in his list, whereas later St. Ildephonse of Toledo (archbishop 657–667) names it *librum de genere officiorum* ("book concerning the nature of offices").[36] In his critical

edition of DEO, Lawson clearly establishes that the original title of
the work is *De origine officiorum (On the Origin of Offices)*.[37] Quite
simply stated, that this is the original title can be shown both by
extensive manuscript evidence and by the structure of each chapter.
As Lawson states, "in each chapter he explains the nature of an
officium, and states when and how it began."[38] In addition, this original title is supported by the many instances where Isidore states his
intention for the work.[39] Despite his conclusion regarding the name,
Lawson continues to use the commonly accepted name, citing the
immense confusion that would result from renaming the work. Thus,
the name of the book used in this translation remains that used in
editions of the work at least since 1534—*De Ecclesiasticis Officiis*. Each
of the present "books" might better be understood as "sections" of
one book.

The work was composed, as Isidore testifies in the book's very
initial lines, at the request of his brother, Bishop Fulgentius. Its purpose is also clear. Isidore provides his brother with an account of the
origin of the various church offices found in the early-seventh-century
Visigothic church.[40] To do so, Isidore follows the same scholarly and
literary style he employs in all his writings. He assembles the biblical
and patristic sources that refer to the topic he is considering, and
then adds his own comments and observations as he judges them necessary or useful. Although Isidore is sometimes described as being a
writer of little talent or imagination, a mere copyist of his sources, the
opposite is true. He consistently adapts and combines his sources with
slight but significant touches for his own purposes. He ends up assem-
bling them in a "veritable mosaic of texts."[41] As carefully documented
by Lawson, there are very few chapters of the DEO in which Isidore's
sources are not adequately attributed.[42]

The book was destined principally for use by clerics, especially
those charged with the pastoral care of the Christian faithful, that is,
bishops. In effect, it is an early example of a pontifical. It is meant to
serve as an official teaching rather than advice, and so Isidore justifies
his compilation by referring to ancient sources. He especially relies on
Augustine's writings. This shows how influential Augustine had
already become in the western churches. The Iberian churches, in
particular, saw themselves linked to the church in northern Africa, as
well as to the Roman church. Hillgarth also notes the link of the
church in Spain to Byzantium and Ireland.[43]

Regarding the title of this book, the term *offices* is used to refer both to the Eucharist and to the Liturgy of the Hours as celebrated in Seville, as well as to the functions and duties within the church. The first use is evident even today in the common reference to the Liturgy of the Hours as the "Divine Office." However, the second usage is less common today.

The first section or book addresses chants, hymns, readings, prayers, ceremonies of the eucharistic assembly, liturgical cycles of the Hours, yearly seasons, and feasts; in other words, that which is generally called liturgical services and the liturgical seasons of the year.

Isidore's description of the Eucharist is detailed. He starts with hymns and chants, justifying nonbiblical hymns by citing Hilary and Ambrose. Their usage is affirmed by IV Toledo in canon 13.[44] The Roman Church in contrast would not permit their use until the twelfth century.[45] Isidore continues by describing biblical readings and their function and then moves to the seven prayers of the *missa,* where he describes their respective intentions.[46]

He follows with the Hours, giving their names and purpose. He especially focuses on the Hours linked to the Paschal Triduum. In this section he also addresses diverse observances of penitential practices, some of which have led to schisms among Christians. This first "book" is completed by a transitional section describing those who are consecrated for church service as well as the role of married people, catechumens, and candidates for baptism.

The second "book" goes into detail about the various roles and functions within the church. Isidore begins with a discussion of clerics, their rules and ranks. He continues with priests, including bishops and presbyters. Then he moves to describe deacons and the minor orders. Next he considers various rankings or groupings of laity in the church. He concludes this section by describing the rites of initiation, including a discussion of catechumens, the symbol and rule of faith, baptism, and chrismation/confirmation.

In terms of clerics, Isidore engages in three diatribes of warnings about their lifestyle, commitments, and obligations to the hierarchy. Isidore also describes the qualities of a good bishop as well as of good monks. It is significant that, at the end of this list, he describes penitents, virgins, and married people as "orders" of the church. It is especially noteworthy that he describes marriage in positive terms despite the vicissitudes of Adam and Eve, the rigorism of Tertullian, and even Ambrose and Augustine, the three principal sources for this section.[47]

The substance of the two sections of DEO is not difficult to understand in terms of the intellectual content. It is like an encyclopedia, which seeks to gather from approved sources descriptive data to explain the origin of things that are of value and commonly used by the Christian community. Nevertheless, Isidore's phrasing and terminology are often confusing owing to the changing use of Latin in this postclassical era.

After this brief overview of the content of DEO, I would now like to return to the topic of the eucharistic liturgy. As I noted above, Isidore's DEO provides the clearest outline of the Visigothic liturgy, one of the major rites comprising the liturgies of the Latin West. In fact, Isidore is credited with providing the foundational structure of this liturgical rite. In order to highlight the major significance of this work, especially since it played such a key role in the updating and renewal of the Hispano-Mozarabic rite undertaken in the late twentieth century, it is important that I now turn to a consideration of the liturgies of the Latin West.

LITURGIES OF THE LATIN WEST

There were nearly seven hundred years of continuous Roman involvement in the Iberian Peninsula, beginning in 264 BC and ceasing only when definitive Visigothic rule was established in AD 415. Romanization left its mark on many aspects of Iberian life in its governmental, social, and cultural institutions. Simon Keay notes that Hispano-Roman civilization was a unique blend of the cultures of those already existing in the peninsula and the culture imposed from authority centered in Rome.[48]

By the time Caracalla granted Roman citizenship to all residents of the empire in AD 212, the Romanization of the Hispanic peoples was completed in a legal sense.[49] The adoption of Roman names, customs, and language took longer. Nonetheless, a large number of Iberians, despite pockets of resistance, considered themselves Roman in many ways by the time of the Visigothic triumph in the fifth century, not least of all in their Christianity. Thus, it is appropriate to refer to them as Hispano-Romans. The growth of the Hispano-Roman church was exemplified in many ways by the renown of the Council of Elvira (c. 314) and the influence of one of its bishops, Hosius of Córdoba (d. 357). Hosius not only was an advisor to the emperor Constantine (d. 337) but presided in the emperor's name at the Council of Nicaea (325).[50] The *acta* of the Hispano-Roman and Visigothic councils of the fourth, fifth, and sixth centuries reveal a church linked by communication with the wider communion of catholic churches while maintaining close relationships particularly with the Apostolic See.

The third and fourth centuries encompass a period of great development in the celebration of the Eucharist among Christians, resulting in the formation of various liturgical families. As for the Latin West, Christianity saw the rise of various Latin-language liturgies between the fifth and seventh centuries. Of importance to this introduction is only one of these rites, the Hispano-Mozarabic rite.

The development of the Hispano-Mozarabic rite was a slow process that had its greatest unfolding during the Visigothic era in the sixth and seventh centuries.[51] The *acta* of the third and fourth councils of Toledo, conducted under the auspices of Kings Reccared (reigned 586–601) and Sisenand (reigned 631–636), give clear evidence of this. Three metropolitan sees had the greatest influence on the development of the rite: Seville, Tarragona, and Toledo.[52] Three bishops—Leander of Seville (c. 540–600), his brother Isidore of Seville, and Ildephonse of Toledo (c. 610–667)—contributed to its formation.

A rite can be seen as marked by a particular system of liturgical celebrations that emerges from a distinctive spiritual heritage and follows an explicit ecclesiastical discipline. The liturgy of Spain developed under the auspices of an autonomous hierarchy according to an explicit ecclesiastical discipline until the Spanish church and its liturgical practices were absorbed by the Roman Catholic Church at the end of the eleventh century. I have referred above to Isidore's key role in this development. The liturgy of Spain can be seen as a rite even though today the native liturgical system of Spain is considered to be one of the three "ritual families" that constitute the Roman liturgical patrimony. The autochthonous liturgical system of Spain has been variously called the Visigothic or Gothic rite because of its greatest development under Visigothic rule beginning in the fifth century, and the Mozarabic rite because of its celebration by Christians in areas under Islamic control from 711 to 1492. These Christians were called *mozárabes* (Mozarabs). Yet others refer to the rite as the Old Spanish rite or the Hispanic rite.

Thus, the ancient rite of Spain is one of several Latin-language liturgical systems that developed in the West after Christianity had been implanted and began to spread throughout the Roman Empire in the first four centuries of the church. The church in North Africa was the first to use Latin in its liturgical system. The Roman rite used Greek at first and, after a period of bilingualism, turned exclusively to Latin.[53] For the most part the local churches of the West in this era looked to the Roman church for guidance in matters of faith on occasion[54] and appear to have imitated some of its liturgical practices, at least prior to the reforms of Gregory the Great (c. 540–c. 604). The Spanish church under the Visigoths began to hold regular councils and to some extent to come to its own decisions in questions of liturgy. Even so, they continued to seek advice on controversial questions, such as Leander's question to Gregory the Great about triple or single immersion at baptism.[55] There are only three Latin-language rites that have endured to this day—the Roman, the Milanese, and the Spanish.

Various political and ecclesial factors contributed to the replacement of the Hispano-Mozarabic rite by the Roman rite throughout the reconquered regions of Spain in 1080 by the Council of Burgos. However, when Toledo was retaken from Islamic control in 1085, King Alfonso VI (1065–1109) permitted the Christians there to retain their rite solely in the existing six parishes. Over the centuries the six parishes were collapsed into two because of demographic changes in the Mozarab population of Toledo and other political factors. The present-day parishes are Santa Eulalia y San Marcos and Santas Justa y Rufina. The ancient liturgy of Spain has been celebrated in these parishes regularly, though on a limited basis, as well as in the Corpus Christi chapel of the Cathedral of Toledo over the centuries. With its official "actualization" in 1988,[56] the rite was renamed the Hispano-Mozarabic rite. This name was chosen in order to indicate the rite's provenance and to honor the Mozarabs who had conserved it.[57]

On the feast of the Ascension 1992, Pope John Paul II celebrated the updated liturgy at St. Peter's Basilica using the new books. This event marked another milestone in the rite's survival. As a public act, it demonstrated the import of this rite as an authentic expression of the official prayer of the church, the liturgy. Even before the actualization of the Hispano-Mozarabic liturgy, its significance was such that it was referred to in the rationale of the reform of the Roman rite occasioned by Vatican Council II. Pope John Paul II acknowledged this fact in a homily given at Toledo in 1982. In his homily, the pope praised the Mozarabic community as "heroic Christians" who have maintained their faith and venerable liturgy over these centuries. He went on to say that "we cannot forget that in the post-conciliar liturgy the chant for the Our Father in all of Spain is precisely that of the Mozarabic liturgy."[58] Indeed, the Mozarabic chant version of the Our Father is also an option offered in the English-language edition of the *Roman Missal* used in the United States.[59] The pope again acknowledged the importance of the rite at the liturgical celebration in 1992 when he said, "The Hispano-Mozarabic liturgy represents an ecclesial as well as a cultural reality that cannot be relegated to the loss of memory if one desires to understand deeply the roots of the Christian spirit of the Spanish people."[60]

DEO AND THE HISPANO-MOZARABIC EUCHARIST

In the effort to update and actualize the Hispano-Mozarabic liturgy, the commission charged with this task turned to the existing liturgical sources. Of major importance among these documents and manuscripts was Isidore's *De Ecclesiasticis Officiis*. Already the first major reformer of the rite, Cardinal Francisco Ximénez de Cisneros (1436–1517) turned to St. Isidore for several reasons. One was the growing interest in antiquities that had been occasioned in Italy by the rediscovery of Roman classical culture. Cisneros, motivated by his humanist leanings, wished to show the antiquity and autochthonous nature of Spanish culture vis-à-vis the Roman.[61] Who better than Isidore, the last Latin father of the church?

Dom Jordi Pinell, OSB (1921–1997), considered the premier expert on the rite during its renewal, catalogued 250 liturgical texts dating from the Visigothic era.[62] He and other scholars have noted that the composition of texts and the creative unfolding of the eucharistic celebration in Spain occurred later than in the other churches of the Mediterranean ambit.[63] The creativity of the Visigothic era was fueled by contact with other churches in both East and West, as can be seen by the incorporation of various elements from their liturgies. Other scholars have noted the abundance and richness of the prayer formulas found in the textual sources: "One can find in them veritable theological theses with all of their developments."[64] Some, however, are also prolix and redundant in character, thereby making them difficult to pray and at times to understand.

The retrieval and study of the ancient manuscripts have led scholars to conclude that originally there was no one manner of celebrating the Hispano-Mozarabic rite.[65] Rather, despite synods calling for uniformity, each of the six metropolitan sees of the early Visigothic era tended to order the celebration and prepare its own texts according to its own purposes. The six metropolitan sees during the Visigothic era were Braga (northwestern Spain, today in Portugal), Cartagena (eastern Spain, today in Murcia Province), Mérida (western Spain, today in Extremadura), Sevilla (southern Spain, today in Andalucía), Tarragona (northeastern Spain, today in Cataluña), and Toledo (central Spain, today in Castilla-La Mancha). Each had suffragan dioceses that incorporated the liturgical and ecclesial practices of its metropolitan. Among all these, the Visigoths made Toledo, their territorial capital, the primatial see at the expense of others perhaps more worthy. Nonetheless, it is reasonable to conclude that, based on the sources, variability was a value for the ancient Spanish church at one time. The "Prenotandos" of the *Missale* (1991) state that the three metropolitan sees of Tarragona, Sevilla, and Toledo were especially influential in the formation of the rite.[66] Eventually the Councils of Toledo III (589) and IV (633), under Leander and Isidore respectively, succeeded in getting the majority of the sees to conform to a basic structure with some important variations.[67] These variations in celebrating the rite were sufficiently pronounced so that "in the sources that have come down to us the existence of two distinct traditions should be recognized."[68]

Two traditions perdured, as evidenced by the textual sources. Pinell recognized an overall structure to the textual variations that have survived. He grouped the surviving texts into two general categories, which the Prenotandos of the *Missale* simply identify as Tradition A and Tradition B.[69] The Prenotandos of the *Missale* note that Tradition A is represented by the majority of the manuscripts and evinces the liturgical uniformity sought in the "northern" and "southeastern" provinces of Tarraconensis and Carthaginensis through the influence of Toledo.[70] On the other hand, Tradition B is exemplified by a few manuscripts apparently conserved by those who migrated to Toledo from Seville, the metropolitan see of the Bætica Province.[71] The names Tarraconensis and Carthaginensis reflect the vestiges of the Roman division of Hispania and represent the northeast, east, and central sections of the Iberian Peninsula, whereas Bætica was the Roman name of southern Spain.[72] These divisions were retained as ecclesiastical provinces under the Visigoths.

Pinell linked the manuscripts conserved and recopied in Toledo by the parishes of Santa Eulalia and Santas Justa y Rufina to these two traditions.[73] Scholars hold that three of the six parishes were associated with the "northern" tradition.[74] These included Santa Eulalia, San Lucas, and San Sebastián. Their usage was erroneously identified with St. Leander. The other three parishes, Santas Justa y Rufina, San Marcos, and San Torcuato, were associated with the "southern" tradition, attributed erroneously to St. Isidore.[75] Pinell judges the manuscripts linked to Santa Eulalia as dating from the period between the eighth and twelfth centuries, which he judges to be more extensive and better organized.[76] The codices linked to Santas Justa y Rufina were probably taken there sometime in the tenth to twelfth centuries when a number of bishops and faithful fleeing from Seville installed themselves in the parish dedicated to the Sevillan saints.[77] Pinell speculates that the surviving texts were copied from the earlier codices and dates them to the period of the fourteenth and fifteenth centuries; for him, this late date implies that the liturgy was maintained with greater zeal in the parish of Santas Justa y Rufina, whereas almost all the other parishes had more or less abandoned their ancestral liturgy.[78]

The texts constituting the northern tradition (A), secured at Toledo, can be traced to a wide zone encompassing Tarragona and Narbonne in the east to León in the west, and from San Millán and Silos in the north, south to Toledo.[79] Pinell hypothesizes that the texts of the southern tradition (B) reflect only the liturgy of Seville.[80] Pinell also points to substantial differences in the two traditions' celebration of Holy Week, as well as in the structure and euchology of the Mass and Office. Both traditions, nonetheless, have many common texts, although they do not often coincide in their order and distribution. In addition, both traditions exhibit completely different systems of biblical readings.

The manuscripts continued to be used in the parishes up to the time of the first major reform of the rite occasioned by Cardinal Cisneros in 1500. The Cisneros reform employed only modified texts of Tradition B for the compilation of the *Missale mixtum secundum regulam beati Isidori dictum Mozarabes.*[81] Ramón Gonzálvez, the chief archivist of the Capitular Archives and Library of the Cathedral at Toledo, believes that most of the manuscripts continued to be kept in the parishes after they were consulted for the Cisneros reform.[82] Nonetheless, by the midpoint of the sixteenth century, moved by the Renaissance, people began to collect ancient manuscripts; at that time the documents began to make their way into the Capitular Library of the Cathedral, where some are still kept.[83] The texts from both traditions were eventually incorporated into the new *Missale.*

The extant texts employed for the actualization of the Hispano-Mozarabic rite come from a variety of sources. Many of the original texts were new compositions that appeared during the fifth and sixth centuries in Spain. Although most of the composers of liturgical texts and chants are unknown, many are known having been transmitted through tradition. They include Justo de Urgell (first half of the sixth century), St. Leander, St. Isidore, Pedro de Lleida (mid-seventh century), Conancio de Palencia (mid-seventh century), St. Eugene II of Toledo (d. 657), St. Ildephonse of Toledo (c. 610–667), and St. Julian of Toledo (c. 642–690). In addition, the names of many of the copyists of liturgical texts are known, since they signed their names to their work.[84]

Once the period of creativity waned, prominent bishops of Toledo began to compile the texts into liturgical books. As occurred with the Roman and Gallican rites, the basis of these texts were individual *libelli* collected for transmission.[85] St. Julian of Toledo (d. 690) compiled the earliest Spanish sacramentary and a number of other liturgical books.[86] This was a decisive step toward liturgical uniformity, at least for the sees related to the capital. However, the invasion of the peninsula in 711 by Islamic peoples and their total domination of it by 719 impelled some clerics to flee to other Christian realms in the West. Apparently they took with them their Spanish liturgical books. Thus, a prayer book for the Office from Tarragona was taken to Verona, where it was deposited in the Capitular Library of the Cathedral.[87] Others found their way into the libraries of northern monasteries.[88] In this way, some texts with a Spanish origin or aspect eventually were incorporated into the Germano-Roman Pontifical.[89]

Christians continued to practice their religion and celebrate the Eucharist in their ancient rite in regions under Islamic control until the fifteenth century.[90] There were organized Mozarab communities throughout most of al-Andalus (southern Spain), most notably in Sevilla, Córdoba, Mallorca, Málaga, Murcia, Granada, and Valencia well into the twelfth century. The same was true until the eleventh century in most of the kingdoms established as the result of the efforts to reconquer the peninsula.[91] Codices and fragments of Hispano-Mozarabic texts coming from some of these areas, copied from the tenth to the fifteenth centuries, have been preserved as well in the Capitular Archives and Library of the Cathedral at Toledo, the Biblioteca Nacional in Madrid, and other museums and libraries. For example, Dom Marius Férotin, OSB (d. 1914), cites the British Museum (London), the Bibliothèque Nationale (Paris), the Library of the Cathedral of León, the libraries of Silos and San Millán, the Biblioteca Nacional in Madrid, the Archives of Compostela, the Archives of Córdoba, the Library of Carmona, the Capitular Archives of Toledo, and the Museo del Hospital de la Santa Cruz as sites where he located Mozarabic rite manuscripts.[92] These sites continue to hold them, as does the Museo de los Concilios y de la Cultura Visigótica in Toledo.

Over the course of the centuries, especially since the Cisneros reform of the rite, other events have helped shed greater light on the textual sources and the conservation of the rite itself. For example, on the cusp of the eighteenth and nineteenth centuries, another cardinal of Toledo, Francisco Antonio de Lorenzana (1722–1804), identified errors in Cisneros's reform and published in Rome a corrected version of Cisneros's missal in 1804 (see *Patrologia cursus completus: Series latina*, ed. J.-P. Migne [Paris, 1844–64], vol. 86). He corrected the earlier edition by consulting the texts from Tradition B (Seville) that were available to him.

Texts from Tradition A (northern) came to light only as a result of scholarly research in the nineteenth century. This research yielded the posthumous publication of the *Liber Mozarabicus* in 1917 by Férotin. Critical work continued on the ancient sources of both traditions through the mid-1900s, which led to the publication of the new *Missale Hispano-Mozarabicum* in 1991. Published in two volumes, it contains the texts from the two traditions, but the updated rite follows the practice of Tradition B (Seville) during ferial days and Lent. In these celebrations, after the entrance of the priest and a simple greeting, *Dominus sit semper vobiscum*, the Liturgy of the Word commences, as evidenced in DEO. The same Tradition B is followed in terms of the structure of the *post anaphora* section of the Eucharist in which the Profession of Faith, Fraction Rite, and Lord's Prayer occur in this order. Thus, the texts of Tradition B make up the bulk of both Cisneros's and Lorenzana's missals as well as the core of the updating of the rite into the 1991 *Missale*. Although texts from Tradition A and other sources were included as options throughout the year, or as a means to fill in missing elements from Tradition B, it is the structure of the eucharistic celebration as found in Isidore's DEO that has been conserved for the contemporary celebration of the rite.[93] Hence, the great significance of this work is obvious.

SOURCES USED BY ISIDORE IN DEO

The sources used by Isidore were first identified by A. C. Lawson in 1937.[94] Christopher Lawson, his son, corrected his father's work and included the list of sources in his critical edition of DEO, published in 1989. Hillgarth notes that Lawson's was the first concerted attempt to trace the whole of the sources for one of Isidore's works.[95] In his analysis, Hillgarth takes note that many North African writers were used by Isidore, including Cyprian of Carthage and Tertullian. Augustine is, of course, to Isidore the greatest of all his predecessors; he is constantly cited. What follows is the listing of the major authors and sources as found in C. M. Lawson's critical edition.[96]

Ambrose: *De Joseph Patriarcha; De officiis ministrorum; Exhortatio virginitatis; Expositio in psalmos*

Augustine: *Confessiones; Contra Faustum; Contra Felicem; De agone christiano; De civitate Dei; De consensu evangelistarum; De cura pro mortuis gerenda; De diversis quaestionibus ad Simplicianum; De doctrina christiana; De genesi ad litteram; De genesi ad litteram imperfectus liber; De genesi contra Manichaeos; De moribus ecclesiae catholicae; De nuptiis et concupiscentiis; De opere monachorum; De peccatorum meritis et* *remissione; De sancta virginitate; De vera religione; Enarrationes in psalmos; Enchiridion ad Laurentium; Epistolae 36, 54, 55, 140, 147, 187, 205; Sermones 9, 45, 172; Tractatus in evangelium Johannis*

Ps.-Augustine: *Sermones 103, 137, 240, 280, 291; Sermo de Symbolo III*

Aulus Gellius: *Noctes Atticae*

Caesarius: *Sermones 192*

Cassian: *Conlationes 10, 18, 21; De institutis coenobiorum*

Codex canonum Ecclesiae Africanae 25

Concilium Agathense: 16, 17

Concilium Antiochenum: 10

Concilium Arelatense II: 5

Concilium Arelatense IV: I

Concilium Carthagenense III: III, 4

Concilium Gerundense: 2

Concilium Neocaesariense: II

Concilium Nicaenum: 4

Cyprian: *De ecclesiae catholicae unitate; De dominica oratione; De habitu virginum; Epistulae 63, 73*

Cyril of Jerusalem: *Catecheses*

Decretum Gelasianum: III, 3

De septem ordinibus ecclesiae

Evagrius: *Altercatio*

Eucherius: *Instructiones ad Salonium*

Eusebius-Hieronymus: *Chronica*

Faustus Reiensis: *De spiritu sancto*

Festus: *De verborum significatione; Fragm. Ex apogr.*

Ps.-Firmicus Maternus: *Consultationes Zacchaei et Apollonii*

Gregory the Great: *Moralia in Job*

Gregory Nazianzus: *De epiphaniis; De luminibus; De Pentecoste*

Hilary: *Instruction psalmorum*

Innocentius: *Epistulae 25*

Jerome: *Adversus Iovinianum; Commentarii in Esaiam; Commentarii in Ezechielem; Commentarii in Ionam; Commentarii in Malachiam; Commentarii in Zachariam; Commentarii in Matthaeum; Commentarii in epistulam ad Galatas; Commentarii in epistulam ad Titum; De viris illustribus; Epistulae 20, 22, 54, 58, 125; Tractatus in psalmos 86, 108*

Ps.-Jerome: *Expositio IV Evangeliorum*

Justinian: *Novellae*

Lactantius: *Divinae Institutiones*

Liber Ordinum

Macrobius: *Saturnalia*

Nicetas: *Ad competentes; De pascha; De psalmodiae bono; De symbolo; De vigiliis*

Origen: *Homiliae in Exodum*

Paulinus Burdigalensis: *Sermo de peaenitentia*

Paulinus: *Vita Ambrosii*

Paulinus Nolanus: *Epistulae 23*

Pelagius: *Ad Demetriadem; Commentarii in epist. I ad Corinthios; Commentarii in epist. I ad Timotheum; Commentarii in epist. ad Titum*

Pliny: *Naturalis Historia*

Prudentius: *Peristefanon.*

Quintilianus: *Institutio oratoria*

Rufinus: *Apologia; Expositio symboli*

Salvianus: *De gubernatione Dei*

Servius: *Ad Aeneidem*

Statuta Ecclesiae antiqua: *93, 95, 96, 98*

Tertullian: *Ad uxorem; De ieiunio; De exhortatione castitatis; De virginibus velandis; De oratione*

Varro: *Gramm. Rom. Fragm.*

Vegetius: *Epitome Rei Militaris*

Vergil: *Aeneis*

Victor Vitensis: *Historia persecutionis Africanae provinciae*

BOOK I
DE ECCLESIASTICIS OFFICIIS.
ST. ISIDORE OF SEVILLE

Sancti Isidori Episcopi Hispalensis, **De Ecclesiasticis Officiis.** Edited by Christopher M. Lawson. [Corpus Christianorum, Series Latina 113, Isidori Episcopi Hispalensis Opera]. Turnholt: Typographi Brepols Editores Pontificii, 1989.

**Here begins the Book
Of Isidore, Bishop of the Church of Seville,
On the Origin of Offices.**

Isidore, to my Lord and servant of God, Bishop Fulgentius.

You ask me for the origin of the offices by whose teaching we are instructed in the churches, so that, by brief references, you might learn in which authors they may be found. Therefore, as you have asked, I have sent the requested little book on the origin of offices, drawn from the most ancient writings of the authors, as space has allowed. I have put many things in it that are of my own composition, and I have included other things that truly are as they were in their writing, so that the reading of the individual items might more easily possess the authority of the faith. Nevertheless, if any of this should be displeasing, my errors will be forgiven more easily, since those things for which the witness of the authors is shown should not be blamed on me.

The Beginning of the Chapters

I. The Church and the Designation of Christians
II. Temples
III. Choirs

THE COMPLETION OF THE CHAPTERS

Those things that are celebrated in ecclesiastical offices are founded partly on the authority of the Sacred Scriptures and partly on apostolic tradition and the established custom of the universal church. And so, as we indicated above, let us refer to the authors to find the earliest sources in which they have arisen.

I. THE CHURCH AND THE DESIGNATION OF CHRISTIANS

(1) The church was first established by Peter in Antioch, and there the name of Christian first arose through his preaching, as the Acts of the Apostles testifies [see Acts 11:26]. They are called Christian, however, by a word derived from the name of Christ. (2) Just as the Jews derived their name from the name of Judah, by whom the dignity of their royal lineage became visible in that people, so also the name of the Christian people has been closely connected to Christ. His privilege among both the gentiles and the Jews is the dignity of dominion.

The church is properly so called,[2] because it calls all people to itself and gathers them as one. (3) It is therefore called Catholic, because it is constituted throughout the entire world; also because it is catholic, that is, general, in its teaching for the instruction of men concerning the visible and invisible things of heaven and earth. It is also called Catholic because it calls the whole human race to the subjection of love and duty toward God, both those who rule and those who are ruled, the learned[3] and the ignorant; and also, finally, it is called Catholic because in general it cures the sins of all people which are committed through the body and the spirit.

II. TEMPLES

(1) The lawgiver Moses was the first to dedicate a tabernacle to the Lord. Then Solomon, having sought for wisdom, established the Temple. After these, in our times, faith has consecrated halls of Christ throughout the world.

III. CHOIRS

(1) Likewise, after crossing the Red Sea, Moses was the first to institute choirs. He separated the ranks into men and women, and then, with himself and his sister walking in front, he guided them in choirs to sing a triumphal canticle to God.

A choir, however, is made in the likeness of a crown and from that is so named. (2) Thus also the book of Ecclesiasticus describes: "The priest is standing before the altar, and round about him a crown of brothers" [Ecclus 50:13].

Characteristically, a choir is a multitude of singers. Among the Jews it consisted of not fewer than ten singers, but among us it consists of an undetermined number from very few to very many without any discrimination.

IV. CANTICLES

(1) Moses also was the first to introduce the canticle. He did so after the Egyptians had been struck by ten plagues and Pharaoh had been submerged with his people. Moses made a joyful exit to the desert through the unaccustomed roads of the [Red] Sea saying: "I will sing to the LORD, for he has triumphed gloriously" [Exod 15:1]. (2) Afterwards Deborah, a not ignoble woman, is reported in the Book of Judges [see ch. 5] to have performed this ministry. Thereafter [it is also reported that] many, not only men but also women, filled with the divine spirit, had sung the mysteries of God.

A canticle is sung by the human voice alone, but a psalm is that which is sung to the accompaniment of the psaltery.

V. PSALMS

(1) The church discloses, in a great mystery, that David the prophet first used the psaltery after Moses [see 1 Chr 13:8; 16:5]. For he, specially selected by the Lord for this duty from childhood, deserved to be both the prince of the singers and the storehouse of psalms.

For this reason, the church frequently uses his psaltery with its melody of sweet songs, by which souls may be moved more easily to compunction. (2) The primitive church, however, so chanted the psalms that it had the psalmist make his voice resonate with only a slight inflection, so that it was closer to speaking than to singing. However, the custom of singing was instituted in the church on account of the sensual ones, not the spiritual, so that, since they do not feel compunction because of the words, they might be moved by the sweetness of the modulation. Thus, in fact, even the most saintly Augustine in the books of his *Confessions* approved the custom of singing in the church, "so that through pleasures of the ears," he said, "the weaker spirit might rise up to the feeling of piety."[4] For in these holy words our souls are moved with more unction and more fervor to the flame of piety when sung than if not sung. I do not know by what hidden familiarity, through the diversity or newness of sounds, all our affections are more stirred when sung by a sweet and accomplished voice.

VI. HYMNS

(1) It is clear that hymns were first written and sung by the prophet David himself, and then also other prophets did so. Afterwards also, the three young men placed in the furnace sang a hymn to the creator of all things, every creature having been convoked. Indeed, we have the example and the commands not only of the prophets but also of the Lord himself and the apostles of how singing hymns and psalms is useful for moving souls and inflaming affection for the love of God.

(2) There are divine hymns, however, and there are those composed by human talent. Hilary the French bishop, born as a Pict, conspicuous in eloquence, was the first one eminent in the lyric of hymns.

After him Ambrose the bishop, a man of great glory in Christ and a most renowned teacher in the church, is known to have shown forth very frequently in song of this kind. Consequently the hymns are called Ambrosian from his name, because they first began to be celebrated in the church of Milan in his time. Because of his fame, from his time on this devout practice is observed throughout the churches of the whole west.

Thus, songs of this type proclaimed in praise of God are called hymns.

VII. ANTIPHONS

(1) The Greeks first composed antiphons, with two choirs alternately singing together like two seraphim and two testaments exclaiming one after another. Among the Latins, however, the same most blessed Ambrose was the first to have instituted antiphons, imitating the example of the Greeks. From that time on their usage has increased in all the western regions.

VIII. RESPONSORIES

Responsories were discovered by the Italians a long time ago. They are called by this name because the choir responds to the one singing in the manner of an echo. Formerly, however, there was only one singer. Now sometimes one, sometimes two or three sing together, the choir responding in many voices.

IX. PRAYERS

(1) Christ both composed and established prayers for us to intercede with the Lord. When, therefore, the apostles sought to entreat with God and did not know how to intercede, they said to Christ: "Lord, teach us to pray" [Luke 11:1], that is, compose prayers for us. Immediately the Lord taught from the book of the heavenly law how they should pray or how they should beseech the Lord.

From this the custom of the church has grown to entreat God by prayers against sorrows of the soul and to use prayers like those that Christ constituted, and like those that the first Greeks began to compose by which the Lord was supplicated.

X. READINGS

(1) Tradition teaches that to proclaim readings is an ancient institution of the Jews. For indeed on the legitimate and prescribed days they used readings from the Law and the Prophets in the synagogues. [The churches of Christ][5] preserve this by ancient institution of the Fathers.

The reading is a not unimportant building up of the hearers. Thus, it is proper that when psalms are being chanted they be chanted by all, that when there is praying all pray, and that when the reading is being read, silence is made, so that it may be heard by all. (2) For even if then someone were to come in while the reading is being celebrated, he would simply adore God and, having marked his forehead, solicitously lend his ear, laying aside his prayer lest he lose the reading. (It is clear that we must pray with all during the time of praying, it is also clear that he can pray privately when he wishes.) We do this because it is not always possible that one have a reading at hand, while the ability to pray is always present. Nor should you think there is little usefulness generated from hearing the reading. (3) Perchance the prayer itself may grow stronger when the mind, filled by a recent reading, runs through images of divine things that it has recently heard. For even Mary the sister of Martha "who listened" more intently to "what he was saying, and sat at the Lord's feet," having neglected her sister, was strengthened by the voice of the Lord [who said] that she had "chosen the better part" [Luke 10:39–42]. Thus also the deacon in a clear voice admonishes silence so that, whether psalms are being chanted or the reading is being read, unity might be conserved by all, so that what is preached to all might be heard equally by all.

XI. THE BOOKS OF THE TESTAMENTS

(1) It is the readings from the Sacred Scriptures that are read in the churches of Christ. The very same Sacred Scripture consists of the

Old Law and the New. The Old Law is that which was given first to the Jews through Moses and the prophets; it is called the Old Testament. It is called a testament because it was written and sealed by suitable witnesses, indeed by the prophets. The New Law is the gospel, called the New Testament, which he gives through Christ the very son of God and through his apostles. (2) That Old Law is, as it were, the root, this New [Law] is, as it were, the fruit of the root. For from the Law it comes to the gospel. Indeed, Christ, who has been manifested in the gospel, was foretold in the Law, or rather he himself spoke in the prophets as it is written: "they shall know that it is I who speak"[Isa 52:6]. He who was sending the Law before as pedagogy for infants, is now presenting the gospel, truly the perfect teaching of life, to all adults. (3) Thus, in the Law the goods of the earth were being promised to those who were working; in the gospel the kingdom of heaven is being offered to those living under grace by faith. The gospel indeed is called the good news, and in truth it is good news inasmuch as those who accept it are called sons of God.

These are the books of the Old Testament, which the leaders of the churches have handed down to be read and received for love of doctrine and piety.

(4) First there are five books of the Law, that is, of Moses: Genesis, Exodus, Leviticus, Numbers, and Deuteronomy. Sixteen historical books follow them: single books of Joshua, son of Nun, namely, and Judges, as well as Ruth; four books of Kings, two of Paralipomenon, two of Esdras, single books of Tobit and Esther and Judith, and two books of Maccabees. In addition to these there are sixteen prophetic books: single books of Isaiah, Jeremiah, Ezekiel, and Daniel, and single books of twelve of the prophets, and these indeed are the prophetic books. (5) After these, there are eight books of verses that are written in a different meter among the Hebrews, that is, the Book of Job, the Book of Psalms, Proverbs, Ecclesiastes, the Canticle of Canticles, the Book of Wisdom, Ecclesiasticus, and the Lamentations of Jeremiah. And thus are completed the forty-five books of the Old Testament.

(6) Of the New Testament first there are the four Gospels: Matthew, Mark, Luke, and John. Fourteen epistles of Paul the apostle follow these. To these also are joined seven catholic epistles of James, Peter, John, and Jude, as well as the Acts of the Twelve Apostles. The

seal of all these is the Apocalypse of John, which is the revelation of Jesus Christ, who concludes all the books both in time and in order.

(7) These are the canonical seventy-two books, and on account of this Moses chose seventy-two [Num 11:24–25][6] elders who were prophesying. On account of this also Jesus our Lord commanded seventy-two disciples to preach. And because seventy-two languages were spread throughout this world, the Holy Spirit fittingly provided that there were as many books as nations by which peoples and nations might be built up to receive the grace of faith.

XII. The Writers of the Sacred Books

(1) These are the writers of the Old Testament according to the tradition of the Hebrews.[7] First, Moses wrote the Pentateuch. Joshua, son of Nun, edited his book. Samuel wrote Judges and Ruth and the first part of Samuel. David wrote the continuation of Samuel all the way up to the end. Jeremiah edited all of Malachi; for previously he was scattered through the histories of the individual kings. The Hebrews think that Moses wrote the book of Job; others think one of the prophets did. (2) Truly ten prophets wrote the Psalter, that is, Moses, David, Solomon, Asaph, Ethan, Idithun, Heman [1 Chr 15:19; 25:1] and the sons of Core, that is Aser, Elcana, Abiasaph [Exod 6:24]; there are those who say they also wrote Esdras and Haggai and Zacharias. Solomon wrote Proverbs, Ecclesiastes, and the Canticle of Canticles. Isaiah wrote his book; Jeremiah wrote his book with his Lamentations. Wise men of the synagogue wrote Ezekiel, the twelve [prophets], Daniel, as well as Paralipomenon and Esther. Esdras wrote his book.

(3) When the Jews had returned to Jerusalem, this same Esdras the scribe, filled with the divine spirit, repaired all these books after the burning of the Law by the Chaldeans. He corrected all the volumes of the prophets that had been corrupted by the gentiles, and he constituted the whole Testament into twenty-two books, so that there were as many books in the Law as there were letters.

(4) Seventy translators edited the first edition after Esdras from Hebrew into Greek under Ptolemy the Egyptian king, the successor of Alexander, who was very studious in reading and gathered together the books of all the nations. For he, sending many gifts to the Temple,

petitioned from Eleazar, who was the high priest, so that six men from the twelve tribes of Israel might be sent over who would translate all the books. And so that he might ascertain the faithfulness of the translation, he gave to each of them who were chosen their own chambers, and assigning the task to all, he ordered that all the writings be translated. (5) Then, engaged in the business of this task for seventy days, the translations of all the writings were completed at the same time. They had made the translations, segregated in different places, none of them close to any other. He gathered them together, and thus all the books were discovered to have been translated through the Holy Spirit, because they were discovered to be consonant not only in meaning but truly also in words. This first translation was true and divine. (6) The churches of all the peoples first began to meditate on these books, and translating them from Greek into Latin, the first providers of the churches handed them down. After this, Aquila edited a second edition; Theodotion and Symmachus, both Jewish proselytes, edited a third and fourth. There was a fifth edition, and then a sixth edition of Origen was found and compared with the other above mentioned editions.

These are thus only the ones who translated the Sacred Scriptures from Hebrew into Greek. These indeed are numbered. (7) Of the Latins who have translated from Greek into our language, as St. Augustine remembers, the number is infinite. "For if to anyone," he says, "during the first times of the faith a Greek codex came to hand and he sensed a little knowledge of his own and the other language, he immediately dared to translate,"[8] and thence it happened that so innumerable were the translators that have existed among the Latins.

(8) Only Jerome the priest, however, translated the Sacred Scriptures from the Hebrew into the Latin language. His edition is generally used by all the churches on every occasion, for the reason that it is more truthful in meaning and clearer in words.

Solomon is proven to have written the Book of Wisdom by these testimonies in which it is thus stated: "You have chosen me," he said, "to be king over your people...and you have ordered me to build a temple to your holy name and [an altar] in the city of your dwelling place" [Wis 9:7–8].[9] (9) The Hebrews, as one of the wise men recalls,[10] accepted this work into the canonical Scriptures. But, after they killed Christ, they comprehended and called to mind the most evident testimonies about Christ in this very book, where it is said: "The wicked said among themselves [Wis 2:1]: Let us seize the just one because he is not useful to us and he is opposed to our works" [Wis 2:12]. And: "He professes to have knowledge of God and calls himself son of God" [Wis 2:13]. And then: "For if he truly is son of God let us seize him and the Lord will free him from the hand of those opposed to him" [Wis 2:18]. And further: "That we might know his reverence and prove his patience let us condemn him to a most shameful death" [Wis 2:19–20]. And thus, lest those of our number diminish them through such an evident sacrilege, they had a meeting, and they removed the book from the prophetic volumes and prohibited their own people from reading it.

(10) Next, Joshua, son of Sirach of Jerusalem, descendant of Joshua the priest of whom Zacharias is mindful [see Zech 3:1], composed the Book of Ecclesiasticus. This book is designated by the title of Solomon among the Latins on account of similarity of language. In addition, it is in no way certain who the authors might be who wrote the books of Judith and Tobit and Maccabees.

(11) Now, in the New Testament, the four evangelists wrote each of the four books of the Gospels. Of these, only Matthew is reported to have been written in the Hebrew language; the rest in Greek. The apostle Paul wrote his epistles. He wrote nine of them to seven churches, the rest to his disciples Timothy, Titus, and Philemon. It is uncertain to most of the Latins if the epistle to the Hebrews is Paul's on account of the dissonance of language. Some attribute its authorship to Barnabas, while others suspect it was written by Clement. (12) Peter wrote the two epistles with his name, which are called catholic. Of these his second is not believed by some to be his because of the difference of its style and vocabulary. James wrote his epistle, which is also denied by some to be his. Rather it is thought to have been written by another under his name. John himself edited the epistles under his name. Only the first of these is asserted by some to be his, the remaining two of John are ascribed to a certain presbyter, who, according to the opinion of Jerome, is proved by a second tomb in Ephesus. Jude edited his epistle. Luke composed the Acts of the Apostles as he heard or saw. The evangelist wrote the Apocalypse of John at the same time as he was handed over, bound, on the island of Patmos for preaching the gospel.

(13) These are the writers of the sacred books, speaking "as inspired by God" and dispensing heavenly precepts "for teaching" [2 Tim 3:16]. However, the author of these Scriptures is believed to be the Holy Spirit. For he himself wrote, who dictated through his prophets what was to be written.

And now, following the origin of the psalms and hymns, and also after the number of sacred books, I will indicate for you the following items you have requested.

XIII. LAUDS

(1) Lauds, that is, the Alleluia, has been sung since antiquity by the Hebrews. Its explanation consists in the translation of two words, that is, "God's praise."[11] John reports about its hidden meaning in the Apocalypse, the spirit revealing himself to him, that he had seen and "heard the voice" of a heavenly company of angels "like the sound of many waters and like the sound of mighty thunderpeals, crying out 'Hallelujah'" [Rev 19:6]. (2) From this no one should doubt that this mystery of praise, if celebrated with worthy faith and devotion, is joined to that of the angels.

Alleluia, as also *amen*, is never translated from Hebrew into another language, not because they are less able to be translated, but, as the teachers[12] say, antiquity is preserved in them because of their more sacred authority.

(3) In African regions, however, the *alleluia* is not sung all the time but only on Sundays and during the fifty days after the resurrection of the Lord as an indication of future resurrection and rejoicing. On the other hand, among us, according to the ancient Spanish[13] tradition, the *alleluia* is chanted always except for fast days or during Lent. For it is written: "his praise shall continually be in my mouth" [Ps 33(34):2].

(4) When the *alleluia* is chanted at the end, after the conclusion of the psalms or the preaching of the readings, the church does this in future hope. It signifies, after the announcing of the heavenly reign, which is preached to the world in this life through both testaments, that our future action is nothing other than the praise of God. For it is written: "Happy are those who live in your house, ever singing your praise" [Ps 83(84):5]. This is the reason that the Book of Psalms

is concluded in praise, so that the same eternal praise after the end of the world might be shown.

XIV. THE OFFERTORIES

(1) The Book of Ecclesiasticus is an indication that offertories, which are sung in honor of sacrifices, were formerly sung only when sacrificial offerings were being immolated. For thus it says: "The priest stretched out his hand in offering and he poured out the blood of the grape and he poured out at the foot of the altar a divine odor to the most high prince. Then the sons of Aaron would exclaim in drawn out tubas and they would sound and they would make a loud voice, heard in remembrance before God" [Ecclus 50:16–18 (Sir 50:15–16)]. No differently even now we lift up chants in the sound of the tuba, that is, in the raising up of the voice. Proclaiming praises to the Lord both in heart and in body, we rejoice in that same true sacrifice, by whose blood the world has been saved.

XV. THE MASS AND THE PRAYERS

(1) The order of the Mass and the prayers, by which the sacrifices offered to God are consecrated, was first instituted by St. Peter. This celebration is realized in one and the same way throughout the entire world.

The first of these prayers is a prayer of admonition directed to the people so that they might be stirred up for the purpose of entreating God.

The second is one of invocation to God that he might kindly receive the prayers of the faithful and their offering.

The third prayer is said for those offering or for the faithful departed that they might obtain pardon through this same sacrifice.

(2) After these, the fourth is offered before the kiss of peace so that, everyone having been reconciled to each other in charity, they might be worthily united in the sacrament of the body and blood of Christ, because the indivisible body of Christ does not accept the discord of anyone.

The fifth then follows, which is the *illatio*[14] for the sanctification of the offering, in which the universe both of earthly creatures and of heavenly powers is called forth for the praise of God, and the *Hosanna in excelsis* is chanted because, the savior having been born of the root of David, salvation will reach from the earth all the way to the heavens.

(3) Next there follows the sixth prayer, which is the confirmation of the sacrament, so that the oblation that is offered to God, sanctified through the Holy Spirit, might be conformed to the body and blood of Christ.

The final prayer of these is that which our Lord instituted for his disciples to pray, saying: "Our Father in heaven" [Matt 6:9]. In this prayer, as the fathers have written, there are contained seven petitions. In the first three there are requested eternal things; in the following four, temporal things, which nevertheless are sought so that eternal things might be gained. (4) Thus, when we say: "Hallowed be your name, your kingdom come. Your will be done on earth as it is in heaven" [Matt 6:9–10; Luke 11:20], these three things are begun here on earth, but they are hoped for fully in that life where the sanctification and the will and the kingdom of God will remain forever in his saints. And next, the daily bread that is granted to both soul and body truly is requested here in this world; here also, after receiving nourishment, pardon is sought according to the manner in which fraternal mercy [is extended]. It is here [in this world] that we ask that we not be led into the temptation of sin; it is here, finally, we implore the help of God that we might be freed from evil. In that place, however, there is nothing of these things. (5) The savior taught this prayer in which there is contained both the hope of the faithful and the confession of sinners. About this prayer the prophet preaching said: "Then everyone who calls on the name of the Lord shall be saved" [Joel 2:32 (Vulgate)].

These, then, are the seven prayers of the sacrifice entrusted to us by evangelical and apostolic teaching. This number appears to have been established either because of the sevenfold completeness of the holy church or because of the sevenfold spirit of grace, by whose gift those things which are offered are sanctified.

XVI. The Nicene Symbol

(1) The Symbol, which is proclaimed by the people at the time of sacrifice, was promulgated by the 318 holy fathers gathered at the synod of Nicaea. This rule of the true faith excels in mysteries of such great doctrine that it speaks about every part of the faith, and there is almost no heresy to which it does not respond through individual words or statements. It tramples on all the errors of impiety and blasphemies of faithlessness, and because of this it is proclaimed by the people in all the churches with equal confession.

XVII. The Blessing of the People

(1) The ancient blessing through Moses announced and established that a blessing be given to the people by priests, by which it is commanded to bless the people under the sign of a threefold invocation. For the Lord said to Moses: "Thus you shall bless my people [the Israelites]: You shall say to them, The LORD bless you and keep you; the LORD make his face to shine upon you, and be gracious to you; the LORD lift up his countenance upon you, and give you peace" [Num 6:23–26].

XVIII. The Sacrifice

(1) Christ our Lord and teacher first instituted the sacrifice, which is offered by Christians to God, when he entrusted his body and blood to the apostles before he was handed over, as it is read in the Gospel: "Jesus took a loaf of bread" and the cup "and after blessing gave it to them" [Mark 14:22]. Indeed, Melchizedek the king of Salem first offered this sacrament figuratively in a type of the body and blood of Christ. He also first expressed the mystery of this great sacrifice, as an image, presenting beforehand the likeness of our Lord and savior Jesus Christ the eternal priest, to whom it is said: "You are a priest forever according to the order of Melchizedek" [Ps 109(110):4]. (2) It is commanded that Christians celebrate this sacrifice, having left behind and finished the Jewish sacrificial offer-

ings that had been commanded to be celebrated during the slavery of the former people. Therefore, that sacrifice is done by us which the Lord himself did for us. His offering took place not in the morning but after eating in the evening. For it was fitting that Christ celebrated it around evening of the day, in order that the hour of sacrifice might indicate the evening of the world.

Consequently, however, the apostles did not partake while fasting, because it was necessary that the prefiguring of the Pasch be accomplished first, and thus they might pass over anew to the true sacrament of the Pasch. (3) This was done, then, in a mystery, that at first the disciples did not receive the body and blood of the Lord while fasting. By the universal church, however, now it is always received by those who are fasting. For thus it has been pleasing to the Holy Spirit through the apostles that, in honor of so great a sacrament, the body of the Lord passes first before any other food into the mouth of the Christian. Thus this custom is observed throughout the whole world.

For "the bread that we break" [1 Cor 10:16] is the body of Christ who said: "I am the living bread that came down from heaven" [John 6:51]; and the wine is his blood, and this is what is written: "I am the true vine" [John 15:1]. The bread, because it strengthens the body, is thus called the body of Christ. The wine, because it acts on the blood in the body, is therefore referred to as the blood of Christ. (4) However, although these things are visible, nevertheless, sanctified through the Holy Spirit, they pass over into the sacrament of the divine body.

This is, however, just as the most holy Cyprian says: "The chalice of the Lord is offered mixed with wine...because we see that people are signified in the water, and truly in the wine the blood of Christ is shown. However, when water is mixed with wine in the chalice, the people are united to Christ, and the multitude of the believers is bound and joined to him in whom they believe. This union and mingling of water and wine is so mixed in the chalice of the Lord that the commingling cannot be separated one from the other, just as the church cannot be divided from Christ. (5) Thus, however, in offering up the chalice of the Lord, water alone cannot be offered, just as wine alone cannot. For, if anyone offers wine alone, the blood of Christ begins to be without us. If, truly, the water is alone, the people begin to be without Christ. But when both are mixed and, joining by being poured together, are united with each other, then the spiritual and heavenly sacrament is completed. Thus, truly the chalice of the Lord cannot be water alone, or wine alone, unless both are mixed together, just as the body of the Lord cannot be wheat flour alone or water alone unless both have been united and joined and made solid in the structure of one bread. (6) By this very sacrament, our people are shown to be united so that, just as many grains collected in one and united and mixed form one bread, so in Christ, who is the heavenly bread, we may know there is one body, to which our number is joined and united."[15]

(7) Some say that the Eucharist ought to be received daily unless some sin comes in the way; for, at the Lord's command, we request that this bread be given to us daily, saying: "Give us each day our daily bread" [Luke 11:3]. They say this well if they receive it with reverence and devotion and humility, and if they do not perform this action, proudly believing in the presumption of their own righteousness. On the other hand, if there are such sins that would move them back from the altar as if dead, penance is to be accomplished first and then this salvific medication is to be received. "For whoever eats in an unworthy manner eats and drinks judgment against themselves" [1 Cor 11:27, 29]. And this is to receive unworthily—if one receives at the very time that one ought to be doing penance. (8) On the other hand, if the sins are not so great that it is judged one ought to be kept from communion, one should not separate oneself from the medicine of the Lord's body, lest, the abstaining person being prohibited for a long time, he would be separated from the body of Christ. It is clear that they live who draw near to his body. Thus, it is to be feared, lest, while one is separated for a long time from the body of Christ, one would remain separated from salvation, the Lord himself saying: "unless you eat the flesh of the Son of Man and drink his blood, you have no life in you" [John 6:54 (Vulgate)]. Thus, whoever has presently ceased from sinning ought not to stop from communicating.

(9) However, marital couples ought to abstain from conjugal union and [they ought] to free themselves for many days of prayer, and thus then approach the body of Christ. Let us read again the Books of Kings [1 Sam 21:4–6]. We will find that the priest Achimelech was not willing to first give David and his sons from the breads of proposition, unless he first had asked whether the sons had been pure from a woman, and not only from another woman but also from their wife. Unless he had heard that they had abstained from the conjugal act since yesterday and the day before yesterday, he would never

have given them the bread, which he had previously denied. (10) How much difference is there between the breads of proposition and the body of Christ? As much difference as there is between a shadow and a body, between the imagined and the reality, between the examples of future things and those things that are prefigured through the examples. For this reason some days should be chosen on which one lives more purely and more continent, so that one can come as a worthy person to such a great sacrament.

(11) We believe that it is a tradition from the apostles themselves that the sacrifice is offered for the repose of the faithful departed or to pray for them, because this is maintained throughout the whole world. The Catholic Church holds this everywhere. For if it did not believe that the faithful departed are forgiven their sins, it would not give alms for their souls or offer sacrifice to God. (12) For when the Lord says: "whoever speaks against the Holy Spirit will not be forgiven, either in this age or in the age to come" [Matt 12:32], he makes clear that there will be some [of the deceased] whose sins are to be forgiven in that place and purified by a certain kind of cleansing, purgatorial fire. Thus, in a certain place it is said by the most blessed Augustine: "Without doubt the souls of the dead are relieved by the piety of their living ones, when the sacrifice is offered for them or they give alms, as long as nevertheless this person prepared some merit for himself while he was still living in the body, through which any of these things they do for him are able to be of value to him. (13) For they are not of value to all people, only because of the different kind of life that the person led while in the body. Accordingly, these [actions offered] are thanksgivings when made for the very good. They are propitiatory offerings when made for the not very bad. And, when made for the very bad, they are consolations of some sort for the living, even if they are of no help to the dead. But for those for whom they are of value, their benefit consists either in that there is a full remission of sin or at least that their damnation will be more tolerable."[16]

XIX. The Third, Sixth, and Ninth Hours of the Offices

(1) Daniel and the three young men devoted the third, sixth, and ninth hour to prayers, so that, from the start of the day, three hours poured out in prayer might demonstrate reverence of the

Trinity to us. This occurred also so that from the third to the sixth and indeed to the ninth hour, through intervals of light determined in fixed dimensions, the Trinity might be worshiped, called upon three times a day. This also occurs as a proof of the blessed Trinity, because the Holy Spirit descended to earth at the third hour, that is, in its own place and number and time, to dispense the grace that Christ promised. (2) Thus also Christ suffered at the sixth hour and he offered up the tortures of the gibbet until the ninth. In such a sign, therefore, by legitimate times for prayer through three hours the perfection of the Trinity is either praised in celebrations or called upon in prayers.

Although also, if the daily celebration is computed through a fourfold office including Vespers, that is, through four three-hour periods, there is signified the world, divided in four parts, saved by the Trinity. Indeed both the stations and military vigils of the night are separated into four parts divided into spaces of three hours, so that in these nocturnal and worldly functions the mystery of the Trinity may be venerated.

XX. VESPERS

(1) Vespers is the end of the daily office and the setting of another daylight. Its solemn celebration is from the Old Testament. It was the custom of the ancients to offer sacrifices and to have aromatic substances and incense burnt on the altar at that time. [David], that hymn-singing witness, performed a royal and priestly office saying: "Let my prayer be counted as incense before you, and the lifting up of my hands as an evening sacrifice" [Ps 140(141):2]. (2) In the New Testament also at this time our Lord and savior first gave to his apostles at supper the mystery of his own body and blood so that the time of sacrifice might indicate the evening of the world. Therefore in honor and commemoration of such great signs, it is fitting for us to attend to the things of God during these times and to proclaim our prayers in worship of him, offering sacrifices to him and equally exulting in his praises.

Vespers is named from the star that is called Vesper. It rises with the setting of the sun, about which the prophet speaks: "And he makes Vesper to shine forth upon the sons of men" [Job 38:32].[17]

XXI. Compline

(1) We also find examples in the fathers that Compline is also to be celebrated, as David the prophet says: "I will not get into my bed, I will not give sleep to my eyes or slumber to my eyelids, until I find a place for the LORD, a dwelling place for the Mighty One of Jacob" [Ps 131(132):3–5]. Who would not marvel at such great devotion of soul for the love of God that he inwardly denied his own sleep—without which human bodies are certainly deficient—until this king and prophet found a place in his heart for building a temple to the Lord? It behooves us to strongly call this thing to mind so that, if we wish to be a place for the LORD himself and we desire that his tabernacle or temple be built in us, we imitate the examples of the saints insofar as we are able, so that it not be said of us what is read: "they sank into sleep; none was able to lift a hand" [Ps 75(76):6].

XXII. Vigils

(1) Concerning the antiquity of vigils, the ancient devotion of vigils is a familiar good for all the saints. Isaiah the prophet calls out to the Lord saying: "My soul yearns for you in the night, my spirit within me earnestly seeks you. For when your judgments are in the earth, the inhabitants of the world learn righteousness" [Isa 26:9]. So also David, sanctified with both the kingly and prophetic anointing, sings: "At midnight I rise to praise you, because of your righteous ordinances" [Ps 118(119):62].

For it was at this time that the destroying angel, passing over, struck down the firstborn of the Egyptians. (2) Hence it behooves us to keep vigil lest we be included in the danger of the Egyptians. The savior warned in the Gospel that he himself would come at these same hours. He was stirring up his hearers to be vigilant saying: "Blessed are those slaves whom the master finds alert when he comes" [Luke 12:37]. "If he comes during the middle of the night, or near dawn, and finds them so, blessed are those slaves" [Mark 13:35; Luke 12:38]. "You also must be ready, for the Son of Man is coming at an unexpected hour" [Luke 12:40]. (3) Jesus did not only teach about vigils by words. He also confirmed it by example. For the Gospel testifies that "he spent the night in prayer to God" [Luke 6:12]. Also Paul and Silas, "in prison, were praying and singing hymns to God, at about midnight, and the prisoners were listening to them, when suddenly there was an earthquake, so violent that the foundations of the prison were shaken. Immediately all the doors were opened and everyone's chains were unfastened" [Acts 16:23–26]. (4) Consequently it behooves us frequently to sing psalms and pray during these hours in holy offices and to look forward to our end, secure, if it should come during such an action.

There is, however, a certain category of heretics who regard vigils, which are sacred and fruitful for spiritual work, to be superfluous, saying that the divine laws that made the night for rest and the day for labor are being violated. These heretics are called νύσταγες in the Greek language, which means "the sleepy ones."[18]

XXIII. MATINS

(1) Concerning the antiquity and authority of Matins, David the prophet is the same witness, saying: "I meditate on you in the watches of the night, Lord, for you have been my help" [Ps 62(63):7–8]; and in another place: "My eyes are awake before each watch of the night, that I may meditate on your promise" [Ps 118(119):148].

Cassian, however, says that the office of the solemnity of Matins was first instituted at a hitherto new time in the Bethlehem monastery where our Lord Jesus Christ deigned to be born of a virgin for the redemption of human salvation.[19] And thus from this the custom of this celebration has become strong throughout the entire world.

(2) Consequently, it was being prayed at dawn so that the resurrection of Christ might be celebrated. For our Lord and savior rose from the dead in the radiant, early morning light, when there began to arise for the faithful the light that, with the dying of Christ, had set for sinners. For this reason also the hope of the future resurrection for all is expected at this same time [of day], when the just and all shall be awakened from this temporary death as if rising from the slumber of sleep.

XXIV. THE LORD'S DAY

(1) The apostles sanctified the Lord's Day by religious solemnity, because on that day our redeemer rose from the dead. Thus, this day

is called the "Lord's" so that on it, abstaining from earthly works and
the allurements of the world, we might serve him only in divine worship, giving honor and reverence on this day, certainly, for the hope
of our resurrection which we have in him. (2) For just as our Lord and
savior Jesus Christ himself rose from the dead on the third day, so also
we hope that we shall be raised in the last age. Hence also on the
Lord's Day we pray standing because this is a sign of the future resurrection. The universal church which is found in the pilgrimage of
mortality does this, looking forward at the end of time to what was
first indicated in the body of our Lord Jesus Christ, who is the "firstborn from the dead" [Col 1:18].

XXV. {THE SABBATH}[20]

(1) The Sabbath was given first to people to be observed bodily
in leisure, so that their bodily form might be at rest. Thus Sabbath is
translated as rest. The Lord's Day, however, was made known not to
Jews but to Christians through the resurrection of the Lord, and from
this its celebration began. For this day, the first to be found after the
seven, is the eighth. Hence, even in Ecclesiastes its significance for the
two Testaments is stated: "Divide your means seven ways for the one,
or even eight" [Eccl 11:2].[21] (2) At first it was handed down that the
Sabbath was only to be observed because formerly it was the rest of the
dead. There had not been, however, the resurrection of the one who
"being raised from the dead, will never die again; death no longer has
dominion over him" [Rom 6:9]. Now after there has been such a resurrection of the Lord in the body, so that there might occur first in
the head of the church what the body of the church hopes for in the
end, the Day of the Lord, that is, the eighth day which is also the first,
came forward in celebration.

(3) This day appears as solemn even in Sacred Scriptures. For
this is the first day of the world: on this day the elements of the world
were formed, on this day the angels were created, on this day also
Christ rose from the dead, on this day the Holy Spirit descended from
heaven upon the apostles. On this day in the desert manna from
heaven was first given. For thus says the Lord: "Six days you shall
gather it, on the sixth day he gives you food for two days" [Exod 16:26,
29]. Thus, the sixth day is the day of preparation that is placed before

the Sabbath. (4) The Sabbath is the seventh day, which is followed by the Day of the Lord on which the manna from heaven first came. Consequently, the Jews may now understand that our Lord's Day is superior to the Jewish Sabbath. It is now clear that the grace of God never descended on them from heaven on their Sabbath but rather on our Lord's Day, on which the Lord first rained down the manna.

XXVI (XXV). THE BIRTH OF THE LORD

(1) The day of the birth of the Lord was instituted by the fathers as the occasion of a prayerful solemnity because on that day Christ willed to be born bodily for the redemption of the world, he who was in the dominion of the Father coming forth from the womb of a virgin.

This is the reason for his having taken on flesh. After that first parent fell, seduced by false hope due to the jealousy of the devil, he, immediately an exile and abandoned, brought forth the root of malice and sin in his entire progeny. Every genus of living things increased more vehemently in evil, evils being spread everywhere and, what is worst of all, the cult of idols. (2) God, therefore, desiring to put an end to sin, looked after us with word, law, prophets, signs, plagues, prodigies. But since even when warned the world did not recognize its errors, God sent his son so that he might take on flesh and appear to humans and heal sinners. He therefore came among the human race because in his own being he was not able to be known by humans. That he might be seen, therefore, "the Word became flesh" [John 1:14], even though, taking on flesh, he was not changed in the flesh. For he took on humanity; he did not lose divinity. The same one is God and the same one is human. In the nature of God he is equal to the Father. In his human nature he was made mortal in us, for us, concerning us; he remained what he was, and he received what he was not, so that he might liberate what he had made.

(3) Therefore this is the great solemnity of the birth of the Lord; this is the new and glorious festivity of this day, the advent of God accomplished for humans. This day is said to be a birthday for the reason that Christ was born on it. Therefore we ought to observe it as a solemn feast each year so that it is called to mind that Christ was born.

XXVII (XXVI). The Epiphany

(1) The apostolic men signified the day of Epiphany with a solemn feast because on that day the star revealed the savior when "wise men came" [Matt 2:2] "to adore" Christ "lying in the manger" [Luke 2:16] offering suitable "gifts" of the Trinity, "gold, frankincense, and myrrh" [Matt 2:11], to the king, who was both God and about to suffer. Therefore they sanctified this day with an annual celebration, that the world might recognize the Lord who brought forth the heavenly elements. (2) On this same day Jesus also was moistened by the baptismal water of the Jordan, and the heavens being parted, he was declared to be son of God by the testimony of the Holy Spirit descending.

The name of this day is called *epiphany* from that which appeared to the gentiles: for "appearance" or "showing" is called "epiphany" in Greek. Therefore this day took its name from these three reasons: that on this day Christ was shown to the people in his baptism, that on this day the star from the east was brought forth for the magi, and that he was manifested to the multitudes by his first sign of turning water into wine.

(3) Cassian reports that among the Egyptians the day of the birth and the solemnity of epiphany are not celebrated in a twofold manner as in the western provinces but rather in a feast of one day.[22] In addition [on this day] letters of the bishop of Alexandria are directed to all the churches and monasteries of Egypt, in which the beginning of Lent and the day of Easter is officially announced.

XXVIII (XXVII). The Day of Palms

(1) The Day of Palms is celebrated because, as the prophet sang, on this day our Lord and savior is reported to have sat on a donkey, heading toward Jerusalem. Then, while going along, a multitude of people with palm branches cried out to him along the way: "Hosanna! Blessed is the one who comes in the name of the Lord—the King of Israel!" [John 12:13]. In the palm branches there was signified the victory that the Lord was about to achieve over death by dying, and that, by the victory of the cross, he was about to triumph over the devil, the prince of death. (2) By sitting on a donkey, however, the one who

came to Jerusalem was revealing the simple hearts of the heathen, which, by presiding over and ruling, he was leading to the vision of peace.

On this day the Symbol[23] is handed over to the elect because of its close proximity to the solemnity of the Lord's Pasch, so that, since they are already hastening to receive the grace of God, they might recognize the faith they are confessing.

The common people call this day the "washing of the heads," because on this day it is the custom to wash the heads of the infants who are about to be anointed, lest perhaps they might come to the anointing soiled by the observance of Lent.

XXIX (XXVIII). The Lord's Supper

(1) The Lord's Supper is the fifth day of the last [week] of Lent, when our Lord and savior, passing from that completed prefiguring of the Pasch to the true Pasch, for the first time handed over to his apostles the mystery of his body and blood. Then, after the heavenly sacraments, the deceitful disciple and traitor accepted the price from the Jews and put the blood of Christ up for sale. On that day also, the savior "got up from the table and began to wash the disciples' feet" [John 13:4–5] in order that the form of humility that he had come to teach would be recommended, just as he subsequently explained. He did this also because it was most fitting that he should teach by doing what he had previously admonished the disciples to observe. (2) For this reason on this day the altars and the walls and floors of the church are washed and the vessels that are consecrated to the Lord are purified.

And on this day also the Holy Chrism is prepared, because two days before Passover Mary arranged to perfume the head and feet of the Lord with oil. And thus the Lord "said to his disciples: You know that after two days the Passover is coming, and the Son of Man will be handed over to be crucified" [Matt 26:1–2].

XXX (XXIX). Good Friday

(1) Good Friday, that is, the sixth day after the Sabbath, is held in solemnity because on this day Christ fulfilled the mystery of the

cross. It was for this reason he had come into this world so that, because we had been struck down on the wood in Adam, we might be healed again through the mystery of the wood. For by reason of this triumph, human insignificance offers an annual celebration to Christ throughout the whole world because of the fact that he deigned to redeem the world by the blood of his passion and to absolve the sin of the world through the cross, death being conquered.

(2) The substance of his divinity did not undergo the injury of this cross but only the nature of the humanity he had taken on. For the passion was of the body; the divinity remained free from injury.

The justification of the Lord's passion is shown in three parts. The first reason is so that Christ might be given as redemption for the guilt of the world and that the ancient enemy might be caught as if on the fishhook of the cross. Hence he would vomit out those he had gulped down, and he would lose the plunder which he had taken, conquered not by power but by justice, not by domination but by reason. (3) The second reason is so that the official teaching of life might be offered to men still to come. For Christ ascended onto the cross so that a model of suffering and resurrection might be offered to us: of suffering for the strengthening of patience, of resurrection for the stirring up of hope. Thus he might show us two lives in the flesh, one laborious, the other blessed: the laborious which we ought to tolerate, the blessed for which we ought to hope. (4) The third reason for taking up the cross is so that the pride of the world and its inflated wisdom might fall down, humiliated, through the seemingly foolish preaching of the cross. So that it might be evident "that God's foolishness is wiser than human wisdom, and God's weakness is stronger than human strength" [1 Cor 1:25].

(5) The apostle Paul also teaches that "with the eyes of your heart enlightened" [Eph 1:18] we ought to know "what is the breadth and length and height and depth" [Eph 3:18] of the cross. Its breadth is the transverse bar of the cross on which his hands were extended; the length, from the transverse bar down to the earth; the height, from the transverse bar all the way up to his head; and the depth truly that which is hidden, buried in the ground. Through this sign of the cross the entire life of the saints is described. (6) For it is said to us: "Take up your cross and follow me" [Matt 16:24]. For it is then that the body is crucified, when "whatever in you is earthly is put to death: fornication, impurity, passion" [Col 3:5], and so on, and, when the

outer person "is wasting away" so that the inner "nature might be renewed day by day" [2 Cor 4:16], the suffering is of the cross. And these, indeed, although they are good works, they are nevertheless still laborious. The reward of these works is rest, and thus it is said: "Rejoice in hope" [Rom 12:12], so that, thinking of our future rest, we may perform even our laborious tasks with joy. (7) The breadth of the cross on the transverse bar of the wood where the hands are fastened signifies this joy. For the work is understood through the hands, the joy of working through the length, for sadness makes shortness. Next, through the height of the cross on which the head is yoked, there is signified the expectation of celestial retribution through the justice of our sublime God. And the "faith working through love" [Gal 5:6] hopes, so that it might be believed that these good works are to be done not on account of the earthly benefits and temporalities of God, but rather on account of that which is above. (8) And now truly by the length on which the whole body is extended, is signified that tolerance so that we might remain long-suffering. Hence, those who bear up are said to be long-suffering. Through the depth, however, which is that part of the wood which lies hidden, fixed in the earth, but thence raises up everything that stands above, are signified the inscrutable judgments of God by which humans are called by God's hidden will to the participation of such great grace, "one having one kind and another a different kind" [1 Cor 7:7].

XXXI (XXX). HOLY SATURDAY

(1) The veneration of Holy Saturday is celebrated because it was on this day that the Lord rested in the tomb. Therefore, Sabbath in the Hebrew language is well translated as "rest," either because God rested on that day, the world having been completed, or because on that day our Lord and redeemer rested in the tomb. (2) This day is also midway between the death and resurrection of Christ, signifying that rest after death of souls from every labor and from all troubles through which there is a passing over through the resurrection of the flesh to that life of which our Lord Jesus Christ has deigned to give a foretaste in his resurrection.

XXXII (XXXI). Easter

(1) Truly the Easter sacrament, which now is celebrated most clearly in the mystery of our salvation, was first celebrated symbolically in the Old Testament when, the lamb being slain, the people of God celebrated the Passover in Egypt. This symbol was completed in truth in Christ who was "like a lamb that is led to the slaughter" [Isa 53:7]. Our doorposts being smeared by his blood, that is, our foreheads being marked by the sign of his cross, we are being liberated from the perdition of this world, as they were from the captivity of Egypt.

We celebrate the day of his paschal resurrection not only for the fact that he rose from the dead on this day, but also for the other sacraments that are signified by it. (2) Because, as the apostle said: "he was handed over to death for our trespasses and was raised for our justification" [Rom 4:25], the passing from death to life has been made sacred in that passion and resurrection of the Lord. For indeed the word *Pasch* is not Greek but Hebrew. It is named *Pasch* not from "passion, suffering"[24] (for *paschein* in Greek means "to suffer [passively]") but from the Hebrew word for "passing over."[25] The evangelist expressed this especially when the Passover was celebrated by the Lord with his disciples: "Jesus knew that his hour had come to depart from this world and go to the Father" [John 13:1]. (3) The passing over therefore from this mortal life into another, immortal, life, that is, from death to life, is honored in the passion and resurrection of the Lord. This passing over is presently accomplished by us through the faith that is given to us in the remission of sins when we are buried with Christ through baptism [see Rom 6:4], in a sense passing over from the dead, from the lesser to the greater, from bodies to spirits, from the conduct of this life to the hope of future resurrection and glory. (4) Therefore, on account of this beginning of the new life to which we are passing over, and on account of that new person that we are ordered to put on and to take off the old, "[c]lean out the old yeast so that you may be a new batch, as you really are unleavened. For our paschal lamb, Christ, has been sacrificed" [1 Cor 5:7]—therefore on account of this newness of life, the first month of the months of the year [Exod 12:2] is assigned to this celebration.[26] For it is called "the month of new things" [Exod 34:18 (Vulgate)].

Since in the whole duration of the world the third time period has appeared now, therefore the resurrection of the Lord is a Triduum [three-day period]. (5) The first time period is before the Law, the second is under the Law, the third is under grace. In this third period, the mystery is now manifested that was hidden in prophetic obscurity. This is also signified in the lunar number; for since seven is accustomed to appear in Scripture as a mystical number for a kind of perfection, Easter is celebrated during the third week of the lunar cycle, that is, a day that occurs from the fourteenth to the twenty-first. (6) But it is not only because it is the third time period that Easter begins the third week, but also on account of the very revolution of the moon. For at that time it is changing from the lesser things to the greater. This fact about the moon seems to us an analogy, teaching that we should pass over from the visible to the invisible and from the things of the body to the spiritual sacraments that more and more we might die to this world and "our life is hidden with Christ" [Col 3:3]. Hence, we should convert every light of our striving that was turned toward inferior things to the superior, to that eternal contemplation of the immutable truth. (7) Easter is observed up until the twenty-first, therefore, on account of the number seven, by which the meaning of completeness is often symbolized. This is also attributed to the church itself on account of the mark of universality, and therefore also John the apostle wrote in the Apocalypse to the seven churches [Rev 1:4]. The church truly still constituted in this flesh of mortality is often called in Scripture by the name of moon because of its changeableness.

Thus truly the anniversary of the day of Easter does not return to the same day of the year (as, consider, the day on which it is believed the Lord was born), this is because of the Day of the Lord and the moon. (8) It is clear on which day the Lord was crucified and was in the tomb and rose. For the observance of these days was joined together by the councils of the fathers and, the whole Christian world being persuaded, it is fitting that Easter is celebrated in this manner. Thus, not only ought we to look forward to the paschal moon but also to the Day of the Lord on which he was raised from the dead. This is the reason that Easter is not returned to the same day of the year. For the Jews observe the "month of new things" and the lunar cycle in the same manner. Our fathers, however, decreed an added day so that our festivity would be distinguished from the festivity of the Jews.

XXXIII (XXXII). The Ascension of the Lord

(1) The solemnity of the Lord's ascension is celebrated because it is remembered that on this day, after the victory over the world, after the return from the dead, Christ ascended into heaven, as it is written: "When he ascended on high he made captivity itself a captive; he gave gifts to his people" [Eph 4:8]. This feast is celebrated each year, therefore, so that it might be called to mind that the humanity of the flesh he assumed was placed at the right hand of the Father by the ascending Lord. Thus we believe that his body is in heaven in the same condition as it was when he ascended. This also the angelic voice bears witness to, saying: "This Jesus...will come in the same way as you saw him go into heaven" [Acts 1:11], that is, in the same appearance and substance of flesh. Without doubt, he gave immortality to his flesh; he did not take away its nature.

(2) The right hand of the Father, at which the Son is believed to be sitting, is not corporeal, which it is wrong to think about God, but the right hand of the Father is the perpetual beatitude that is promised to the saints in the resurrection, that is, to the whole church which is the body of Christ. In the same way, his left hand is correctly understood as the miseries and eternal punishment that will be given to the wicked.

XXXIV (XXXIII). Pentecost

(1) Certainly the origin and cause of the feast of Pentecost must be traced a little more profoundly. For the day of Pentecost received its start when the voice of God was heard calling down from on Mount Sinai and the Law was given to Moses. In the New Testament, however, Pentecost began when the advent of the Holy Spirit, whom Christ had promised, was shown. He had said that the Spirit would not come unless he had first ascended into heaven. (2) Therefore, when Christ had entered the gate of heaven, ten days having passed, suddenly the place shook where the apostles were praying and, the Holy Spirit descending upon them, they were so inflamed that they "were speaking in the languages of all peoples about God's deeds of power" [Acts 2:11]. Therefore the advent of the Holy Spirit from heaven upon the apostles in a wide variety of languages has been

handed over into posterity, and for this reason Pentecost is celebrated and this day is still of note.

(3) This feast of the Gospel, however, is in harmony with the feast of the Law. Then, after the lamb was immolated, fifty days having passed, there was given to Moses the Law written by *the finger of God.* Now, after Christ was killed, "like a lamb that is led to the slaughter" [Isa 53:7], the true Passover is celebrated and, fifty days having passed, there is given the Holy Spirit who is *the finger of God* upon the one hundred and twenty disciples constituted by the number of the Mosaic era.

And in addition, this feast gains another symbol. (4) For it comes from the seventh of sevens.[27] Indeed, these seven times seven[28] days generate this Pentecost, on which there comes the remission of sins through the Holy Spirit. Truly the seven times seven years make the fiftieth year, which among the Hebrews is called the jubilee, during which similarly there comes the remission of the land and liberty of slaves and restitution of possessions that had been obtained at a price. For seven multiplied seven times produces from itself the number fifty, the number one being assumed, which authority teaches is assumed, from the symbol of the future age, to be greater. For this [day] is always both the eighth and the first, or rather this day is always one [the same] which is every day [of the Lord]. (5) It is necessary that the Sabbath rest of the souls of the people of God take place and then be completed when the portion is given to those eight [days], as he[29] discussing the sayings of Solomon wisely explained [cf. Eccl 11:2].

For this reason, abstinence having been canceled, all of the fifty days after the resurrection of the Lord are celebrated only in joy on account of the symbol of the future resurrection when there will not be labor but the relaxation of joy. (6) Therefore during these days there is no kneeling in praying because, as one of the wise ones says,[30] kneeling is an indication of penance and sorrow. Whence also during these days in all things we observe the same solemnity as on Sunday, on which our elders taught that, out of reverence for the resurrection of the Lord, there is to be neither penance nor kneeling.

XXXV (XXXIV). The Feasts of Martyrs

(1) The fathers of old consecrated the feasts of apostles or the solemnities in honor of martyrs to be celebrated in the sacramental

act of veneration, either for the purpose of stirring up imitation, or so that we might be associated with their merits and helped by their prayers. So therefore we erect altars not to any of the martyrs but to the God himself of the martyrs, although in memory of the martyrs. (2) For which of the witnesses assisting at the altar in the places of the bodies of the saints has ever said, "We offer to you, Peter," or "Paul," or "Cyprian"? On the contrary, what is offered, is offered to the God who crowned the martyrs, in the midst of the memorials of those whom he crowned, so that from the admonition of those places, a greater devotion might spring up, to stimulate love both for those whom we are able to imitate and for the one by whose help we are able to do so. (3) Therefore we honor the martyrs by that cult of love and fellowship in which even in this life are honored the holy men of God whose heart we judge had been prepared for such suffering for the truth of the gospel. But [we honor] the martyrs more devoutly since they are more secure, all uncertainties having been conquered. How much more confidently we preach in praise of the ones already happier victors in [eternal] life, than we do of those who are still fighting in this one.

(4) But truly, we do not honor nor do we teach that anyone be honored by that cult (which is called *latria* in Greek, but which cannot be expressed in one word in Latin), except the one God, since he is served by that which is properly owed to the divinity. And since the offering of sacrifice pertains to this cult (whence idolatry is ascribed to those who show this worship to idols), in no way do we offer or direct to be offered anything like this to any martyr or to any holy soul or to any angel. Whoever slips into this error is reproached through sound doctrine either that he might be corrected or that he might be warned. These saints or men or angels do not wish to have shown to them what they know to be owed to the one God. (5) This was clear in the case of Paul and Barnabas when, excited by the miracles that had been accomplished by these two, the Lycaonians wanted to sacrifice to them as gods. Having torn their vestments, confessing and persuading them that they were not gods, they prohibited these things from being done to them. This was clear also in the case of the angels, as we read in the Apocalypse that an angel was prohibiting that he be adored and saying to the one adoring him: "I am a fellow servant with you and your comrades. Worship God!" [Rev 22:9]. Rightly it is writ-

ten to us that we are prohibited by the angel to adore anyone but the one God, under whom we are also only fellow servants.

(6) Therefore there may not be among us that cult of divine religion directed to the angels or the martyrs, because they are not found to wish such honors as God. They themselves do not wish to be honored as God, but they wish him to be honored by us, rejoicing in his illumination. Therefore the martyrs are to be honored for the sake of imitation. They are not honored for the sake of worship; they are honored out of love, not servitude.

XXXVI (XXXV). DEDICATIONS

(1) We read in the Gospel that annual festivities of the dedication of churches are to be celebrated according to the custom of the elders, where it is said: "At that time the festival of the Dedication took place in Jerusalem" [John 10:22]. Obviously this dedication feast was that of the dedication of the Temple. In Greek the word "new" is *cenon*.[31] Whenever anything new was dedicated it is called *encenia,* a dedication. The Jews solemnly celebrated that day on which the Temple was dedicated, and this day was a feast among them. Even if this custom faded among them because they were without both cult and Temple, Christians keep this custom of the fathers, in whom it seems the honor has been passed down.

(2) All the festivities have been instituted by prudent men for a variety of religious motives and at diverse times in honor of the martyrs, lest there be the rare chance that a congregation of people might diminish its faith in Christ. On account of this, therefore, some days have been so constituted that all might come together as one at the same time so that from a changed outlook their faith might grow and greater joy might arise.

XXXVII (XXXVI). THE FAST OF LENT

(1) According to the Sacred Scriptures there are four times of fasting during which the Lord is to be supplicated through abstinence and the lament of penance. Although it is allowed to pray on all days

and to abstain if it is fitting, nevertheless at these times it is fitting to be devoted to greater fasting and penance.

The first of these is the Lenten fast. This began from the Old [Testament] books with the fasting of Moses [Exod 34:28] and Elias [1 Kgs 19:8], and from the gospel because the Lord fasted [Matt 4:2] on just as many days, demonstrating that the gospel does not dissent from the Law and the Prophets. (2) Of course, the Law is received in the person of Moses, the prophets in the person of Elias. Christ appeared between them in glory on the mountain, so that it might stand out more obviously what the apostle said concerning him: "it is attested by the law and the prophets" [Rom 3:21].

In what part of the year, therefore, would the Lenten observance fit more congruently, except adjacent and contiguous to the Lord's passion—because in it is signified this laborious life, in which also our work is self-control, so that we might fast from the allurements of this world, living on manna alone, that is, on heavenly and spiritual precepts.

(3) By the number forty, in addition, this life is symbolized because money is the perfection of our happiness.[32] (The created world, which depends on the Creator, however, is symbolized by the number seven, in which the unity of the Trinity temporally announced throughout the whole world is declared.) [The number forty also symbolizes this life] because the world is beaten on by the four winds and arises from the four elements and is varied by the changes of the four seasons. Ten calculated four times totals forty. By this number is shown that we are to abstain and fast from every pleasure of the times and live chastely and with continence.

(4) Yet another hidden meaning of this sacrament may be drawn from the fact that these fasts are celebrated for forty days. By the Mosaic Law it was ordered to the whole people in general that tithes and firstfruits be offered to the Lord God. Therefore, although in this statement we are admonished to give back in gratitude to God the first parts of the free-will [offerings] and the fruits of our works, in the calculation of Lent this highest obligation of tithing is fulfilled (the whole time of the year [365 days] divided by the number ten into thirty-six days), the Sundays, on which fasting is canceled, having been subtracted from the forty days. We rush together to church on these days as a tenth of the whole year, and we offer the work of our actions to God in a sacrifice of rejoicing.

(5) As our Cassian says,[33] those who are perfected are not held to this law of Lent, nor are they content with the little subjection of this canon. The leaders of the churches have determined these things for those who really are entangled through the space of the year by worldly pleasures and business. Thus, constricted by this somewhat legal necessity, either they might be forced to be free for the Lord at least during these days, or they might dedicate to the Lord a tenth of the days of their life, all of which would have been devoured as if they were fruit.

XXXVIII (XXXVII). The Fast of Pentecost

(1) The second fast is that which according to the canons starts on another day after Pentecost, according to what Moses says: "You shall count seven weeks; begin to count the seven weeks from the time the sickle is first put to the standing grain" [Deut 16:9].

On the authority of the gospel, this fast is fulfilled by very many after the ascension of the Lord, accepting as historical that testimony of the Lord where he says: "The wedding guests cannot mourn as long as the bridegroom is with them, can they? The days will come when the bridegroom is taken away from them, and then they will fast" [Matt 9:15]. (2) For they say that after the resurrection of the Lord, for those forty days in which it is afterwards written he was in conversation with the disciples, we ought not fast nor mourn, because we are in joy. After that time was completed, when Christ, flying to heaven, withdrew in his corporeal presence, then a fast is to be proclaimed so that through humility of heart and abstaining from meat we might merit to receive the Holy Spirit promised from heaven.

XXXIX (XXXVIII). The Fast of the Seventh Month [September]

(1) The third fast is that which was performed by the Jews after the solemnity of Tabernacles. The church celebrates this on the tenth day of the month of September.[34] This was first instituted in the Law by the Lord saying to Moses: "Tell the Israelites [Lev 23:24]: Now, the tenth day of this seventh month is the day of atonement; it shall be a

holy convocation for you: you shall deny yourselves [Lev 23:27]. For anyone who does not practice self-denial during that entire day shall be cut off from the people. And anyone who does any work during that entire day, such a one I will destroy from the midst of the people" [Lev 23:29–30]. (2) The book of Esdras recalls that the ancients had used this fast: "For after the sons of Israel had returned," he says, "to Jerusalem, and made for themselves a great joyful Feast of Tabernacles, on the twenty-fourth day of this month the people of Israel were assembled with fasting and in sackcloth, and with earth on their heads. Then they...stood and confessed their sins and the iniquities of their ancestors. They stood up in their place and read from the book of the law of the LORD their God for a fourth part of the day, and for another fourth they made confession and worshiped the LORD their God" [2 Esdr (Neh) 9:1–3].

(3) During this seventh month, according to the computation, the sun begins to make the day shorter and the night longer. It is eight days before the first day of October, when the equinox occurs. Therefore a fast occurs in this month, because it is shown in the departing of the sun and the augmenting of the night that our life is growing shorter and death is drawing closer—that death which is restored by the judgment of God and the resurrection.

XL (XXXIX). THE FAST OF THE FIRST DAY OF NOVEMBER

(1) The fourth fast is on the first day of November, which testimony declares was either initiated or instituted by Jeremiah the prophet on divine authority, the Lord saying to him: "Take a scroll and write on it all the words I have spoken to you against Israel, Judah, and all the nations,...perhaps...they will turn back each from his evil way, so that I may forgive their wickedness and their sin. So Jeremiah called Baruch, son of Neriah, who wrote down on a scroll, as Jeremiah dictated, all the words which the LORD had spoken to him. (2) Then Jeremiah charged Baruch...Do you go on the fast day and read publicly in the LORD's house the LORD's words from the scroll you wrote at my dictation...Perhaps they will lay their supplication before the LORD and will all turn back from their evil way; for great is the fury of

anger with which the LORD has threatened this people. Baruch, son of Neriah, did everything the prophet Jeremiah commanded; from the book-scroll he read the LORD's words in the LORD's house. In the ninth month...a fast to placate the LORD was proclaimed for all the people of Jerusalem..." [Jer 36:2–9]. By means of this authority of the divine Scriptures, the church has received the custom and celebrates a universal fast by this observance.

XLI (XL). THE FAST OF THE FIRST DAY OF JANUARY

(1) The church instituted the fast of the first day of January on account of the error of paganism. It was Janus, that ruler of the pagans, from whose name the month of January was named. Ignorant men, honoring him as if he were a god, handed him down[35] to posterity in a religious sense of honor, and they sanctified that day with stage productions and luxuries. (2) During this time, however, miserable people and, what is worse, even the faithful, taking on strange appearances, are transformed in the appearance of wild beasts. Others, changed by a feminine bearing, represent their masculine features as those of a woman. Some even, in a fanatic custom, are profaned by the observation of auguries on this day. They make a lot of noise in everything they do, leaping around and clapping their hands in dancing. By all these things the wickedness becomes more disgraceful, groups bonding between themselves and between both sexes, stripped of spirit, out of their mind with wine, the turmoil is all mixed together. (3) The holy fathers, therefore, observing that the greatest part of the human race was caught up in these sacrileges and bodily pleasures on this day, decreed a public fast in the whole world throughout all the churches, through which people might recognize that they were acting perversely to such an extent that it was necessary in all the churches to fast for their sins.

XLII (XLI). THE CUSTOM OF THE THREE-DAY FAST

(1) Fasting for three days has been taken from the example of the people of Nineveh. Having rejected their earlier vices, they all

gathered together for three days of fasting and penitence and, covered in sackcloth, they prayed to God for mercy.

XLIII (XLII). THE FASTS OF DIVERSE DAYS AND TIMES

(1) In addition to these, however, there are legitimate times of fasting. Every sixth day [Friday] is a day of fasting for some because of the passion of the Lord. Also the day of Sabbath has been consecrated as a day of fasting by many because that was the day on which Christ lay in the tomb, certainly lest that day on which Christ suffered by dying be presented to the Jews as a day of rejoicing. On Sunday, however, there is always eating so that we might proclaim the resurrection of Christ and our joy to the nations, especially since the apostolic see keeps this rule.

(2) After Easter, moreover, up to Pentecost, even though the tradition of the churches permits the rigor of fasting from foods to be relaxed, if any of the monks or clerics desire to fast they are not prohibited, because both Anthony and Paul and others of the ancient fathers, even during these days, are reported to have fasted in the desert and never to have relaxed abstinence except only on Sunday. (3) Who would not praise frugality, who would not preach fasting? For fasting is a holy thing, a heavenly work, the gates of the kingdom, the form of the future life. Whoever does it is joined to the holy God, separated from the world, made spiritual. Through it vices are put down, the flesh is humbled, and the temptations of the devil are conquered.

XLIV (XLIII). THE VARIOUS PRACTICE OF THE CHURCHES

(1) There are these and many other things that arise in the churches of Christ. Of these there are some that are commended in the canonical Scriptures, and there are some that are not indeed written but nevertheless are kept by tradition. But those things that are preserved by the whole world are understood to have been set down

either by the apostles themselves or by the authority of the principal councils. These include the passion of the Lord and the resurrection and the ascension into heaven and the coming of the Holy Spirit, which are celebrated as a memorial during the course of the year, and whatever else is observed by everyone, wherever the church spreads itself. (2) There are other things, truly, that are observed in various ways in different locations, such as the fact that some fast on the Sabbath, some do not. Some go to communion daily, others only on certain days. In some places no day passes on which the sacrifice is not offered; in some places only on the Sabbath and Sunday; in some places only on Sunday. And if there is anything else of this kind that it is possible to recognize, they have instituted this whole realm of things in order that it might seem proper to those priests of the church or region over which they presided. Nor is there any better discipline in these things for the serious and prudent Christian, except that he acts in that manner in which it seems that the church acts, to which he by chance has arrived. For that which is neither against the faith nor against good morals can be followed indifferently and is to be preserved for the sake of the fellowship of those among whom it is observed, lest schisms be generated by initiating differing practices in that church.

XLV (XLIV). The Eating of Meats and Fish

(1) After the Flood, it was permitted that meats and wine be in use by people. For in the beginning nothing had been permitted except only that which was written: "See, I have given you every plant yielding seed...and every tree with seed in its fruit; you shall have them for food" [Gen 1:29]. Afterwards truly through Noah all animals were given for eating, and then permission was extended to wine. But after Christ, who is the beginning and the end, appeared, that which he prohibited in the beginning he also held back in the end times, speaking through his apostle: "it is good not to eat meat or drink wine" [Rom 14:21], and further: "the weak eat only vegetables" [Rom 14:2].

(2) It is not because meats are evil that they are prohibited, but because banquets of these things produce pleasure of the flesh. They

are the nourishment and the nutriment of all the vices: "Food is for the stomach and the stomach for food," as it is written, "and God will destroy both one and the other" [1 Cor 6:13].

We are certainly able to eat fish, because the Lord accepted one after the resurrection. Neither the savior nor the apostles have forbidden this.

This finishes Book I

BOOK II
DE ECCLESIASTICIS OFFICIIS.
ST. ISIDORE OF SEVILLE

The Second Book Begins

Because in the other part we have explained the origins and causes of the offices that are celebrated in common by the church, let us without interruption set forth in an orderly fashion the beginnings of those who carry out the ministries of religion in the divine cult.

THE CHAPTERS BEGIN

The Chapters End

I. Clerics

(1) All who are ordained in grades of ecclesiastical ministry are generally called clerics.

Our teachers say that clerics, or those henceforth called clerics, are so named because we read that Matthias, chosen by lot, was the first who was ordained by the apostles [see Acts 1:26]. Also all those whom the leaders of the churches ordained in those times were chosen by lot. For lot is translated as "cleric." Hence also inheritance is called *klēronomia*[2] in Greek, and an heir *klēronomos*.[3] (2) In like manner, therefore, they say that clerics are named by the fact that they are provided for in the "portion" of the Lord's inheritance, or by the fact that the Lord himself is their lot, as it is written concerning them, the Lord speaking: "I am your share and your possession" [Num 18:20]. Therefore it is fitting that those who possess God as their inheritance endeavor to serve God without any worldly impediment, and that they strive to be "poor in spirit" [Matt 5:3], so that they might be able to say, in accord with the psalmist: "The LORD is my chosen portion and my cup; you hold my lot" [Ps 15(16):5].

II. Rules of Clerics

(1) Clerics, therefore, secluded from ordinary life, are warned by the law of the fathers that they ought to keep themselves free from the sensual pleasures of the world, that they are not to take part in

spectacles or parades, that they are to flee from public banquets, that they are to live a private life, not only chaste but sober.

They should never be inclined to usury, they should never strive for occupations of shameless profits and the pursuit of deceptions of any kind, and they should flee the love of money as the root of all evils. They should give up secular offices and business; they should not seek after positions of honor through ambitions. (2) They should not accept gifts for the benefits of divine healing.

They should beware of trickeries and conspiracies. They should flee hatred, rivalry, detraction, and jealousy. They should not go about with wandering eyes, nor unbridled or petulant tongue and inflated manner, but they should show modesty and reverence of mind, walking in a simple manner. They should completely disavow obscenity both of words and of actions. (3) They should avoid overly frequent visits of widows and virgins; they should in no way seek the companionship of unrelated women. They should strive to preserve chastity, perpetually inviolate of body, or at least they should be bound by the bond of one marriage. They should offer the obedience owed to their elders, and they should not exalt themselves by any desire to show off.

Finally, they should apply themselves to continual training in doctrine, in readings, psalms, hymns, and canticles.

They ought to be such people who strive to have delivered themselves up to divine worship, so that as they give effort to knowledge they may administer the grace of their learning to the people.

III. CLASSES OF CLERICS

(1) There are two classes of clerics: one of ecclesiastics living under episcopal direction, the other of unattached[4] ones, that is, without a head, not knowing whom they follow.

Neither the pursuits of worldly obligations, as among the laity, nor of divine religion, as among the clerics, hold these latter ones fast. Rather a solitary, shameless, and wandering life embraces them, unfettered and wandering about. (2) Since they pursue the freedom of their own satisfied pleasure, fearing nothing, these clerics are carried about by freedom and their own desire like brute animals. Having the sign of religion but not the responsibility of religion, like the centaur they are neither horses nor men, "a mixed breed and a hybrid off-spring" as Virgil says.[5]

Our western region, indeed, abounds in their more-than-sufficient sordid and infamous number.

IV. TONSURE

(1) The use of ecclesiastical tonsure, unless I am mistaken, arose among the Nazirites. At first they maintained their hair; then, through a life of great continence, they shaved their heads in complete devotion and were ordered to place their hair in a fire of sacrifice, so that they might consecrate the perfection of their devotion to the Lord. The use of their examples was introduced by the apostles, so that those who, having been given over to divine worship, are consecrated to the Lord as the Nazirites, that is, the holy ones of God, might be renewed by having their hair cut. (2) Even Ezekiel the prophet was ordered to do this by the Lord speaking: "And you, O mortal, take a sharp sword; use it as a barber's razor and run it over your head and your beard" [Ezek 5:1]. This was because he was serving God devotedly in the manner of a priest in the ministry of sanctification. We also read in the Acts of the Apostles [see 18:18] that those Nazirites Priscilla and Aquila had done this first, and, after them, the apostle Paul and those of the disciples of Christ who stood out by following along in this cult.

(3) Among clerics, however, tonsure is a certain kind of sign that is symbolized in the body but is performed in the soul, so that by this sign in religion vices might be curtailed and we might cast off the crimes of our flesh just like our hairs. Then, senses, like wild locks of hair, having been made new, we might shine forth, according to the apostle, "seeing that you have stripped off the old self with its practices and have clothed yourselves with the new self, which is being renewed...according to the image of its creator" [Col 3:9–10]. It is fitting that this renovation be accomplished in the mind but be demonstrated on the head, where that mind is known to dwell.

(4) Since truly, the head having been shorn above, the crown of the circle is relinquished below [in the mind], I think that the priesthood and the leadership of the church are symbolized in these ways. For among the elders a tiara was placed on the head of the priests.

(This tiara, made out of fine linen, was round in the manner of a sphere.) This is signified in the tonsured part of the head; for the width of the circle is a gold crown which girds the heads of the kings. And either sign [the tiara or the tonsure] is expressed on the head of the clerics so that there might be accomplished by a certain corporal similitude what is written by Peter the apostle emphatically teaching: "you are a chosen race, a royal priesthood" [1 Pet 2:9].

(5) It is asked, however: why as among the ancient Nazirites is the hair not first grown long and then cut. But those who investigate this might pay attention to what is between that prophetic veil and this revelation of the Gospel about which the apostle says: "when one turns to the Lord, the veil is removed" [2 Cor 3:16]. For what that veil placed between the face of Moses and the sight of the people of Israel signifies, that is also what the hair of the saints signifies in these times. For even the apostle says that the hair is like a veil. Therefore it is now not fitting that the heads of those who are consecrated to the Lord be hidden by hair, but rather that they be revealed, because what was hidden in the sign of the prophet is now made known in the Gospel.

V.[6]

(1) Let us come now to the most sacred orders of clerics and we will demonstrate their origin individually.

(V). PRIESTS

What is the foundation of the priesthood or from which founder did the order of bishops arise in this world? Clearly Aaron was the beginning of the priesthood. Although Melchizedek offered sacrifice prior to him and Abraham, Isaac, and Jacob after him—these men did so by spontaneous will, not by the authority of priesthood. (2) In addition, Aaron was the first one in the Law to accept the name of priest, and the first to offer sacrifices, adorned with the distinct priestly stole. For the Lord ordered and said to Moses: "You shall bring Aaron and his sons to the entrance of the tent of meeting, and wash them with water. Then you shall take the vestments, and put on Aaron the tunic

and the robe of the ephod, and the ephod, and the breastpiece, and
gird him with the decorated band of the ephod; and you shall set the
turban on his head, and put the holy diadem on the turban. You shall
take the anointing oil and pour it on his head and anoint him. Then
you shall bring his sons, and put tunics on them, and you shall gird
them with sashes and tie headdresses on them; and the priesthood
shall be theirs by a perpetual ordinance" [Exod 29:4–9][7]

(3) In this place it ought to be considered that Aaron had been
the high priest, that is, the bishop. His sons had ministered beforehand as a type of the presbyters. They were the sons of Aaron and
priests themselves, to whom the Levites had rightly been bound to
minister as also to the high priest. But there was another difference
between Aaron the high priest and the sons of Aaron, who themselves
were also priests: Aaron, over the tunic, received the poderem,[8] the
holy stole, and the gold crown miter and the gold bracelet and the
ephod, and the other things that were mentioned above. The sons of
Aaron, however, over the linen tunics had only cinctures and tiaras,
when they were offering sacrifice to God. (4) But perhaps this might
also be asked: of whom was Moses acting as a type? For if the sons of
Aaron were acting as a type of the presbyters and Aaron of the high
priest, that is, of the bishop, then of whom was Moses? Without doubt,
of Christ, and truly Christ in every way, because he was the symbol of
the mediator of God who is between God and man—Jesus Christ [see
1 Tim 2:5], who is the true leader of the peoples, the true chief priest
and lord of the bishops, to whom are honor and glory forever and
ever [cf. Ps 28(29):2; Rev 5:13]. Amen.

(5) Thus far concerning the first priests in the Old Testament.
In the New Testament, however, after Christ the order of priesthood
began with Peter. For to him the pontificate in the church of Christ
was given first. Thus the Lord said to him: "you are Peter, and on this
rock I will build my church, and the gates of Hades will not prevail
against it. I will give you the keys of the kingdom of heaven" [Matt
16:18–19]. He was therefore the first to receive the authority of binding and loosing, and the first to bring people to faith by the power of
his preaching. And since the other apostles also became equal sharers
with Peter in honor and authority, they also preached the gospel, dis-
persed throughout the whole world. (6) Coming after them, there
succeeded them the bishops, who have been set up throughout the
world in the seats of the apostles. They are not chosen now from

descent by flesh and blood [cf. Ps 44(45):17], which was done first according to the order of Aaron, but by each one's merit, which divine grace has bestowed on him. Thus also the Lord proclaimed to Eli, saying: "Therefore the LORD the God of Israel declares: 'I promised that your family and the family of your ancestor should go in and out before me forever'; but now the LORD declares: 'Far be it from me; for those who honor me I will honor, and those who despise me shall be treated with contempt'" [1 Sam 2:30].

(7) There are four kinds of apostles: the first is from God, as in the case of Moses. The second is through man and God, as Joshua. The third is only through man, since in these times many are called into the priesthood because of the approval of people and authorities. The fourth, however, is a category unto itself, as of pseudo-prophets and pseudo-apostles. As for the name of apostles, however, in the Latin language *apostles* is translated as "sent" because Christ sent them to evangelize for the illumination of all peoples.

(8) The episcopate, however, as one says more cautiously, is a name of a work, not of an honor. It is a Greek word, and from it is taken the word that signifies that he who is placed above superintends or takes care of those whom he governs. *Scopos,* indeed, is "intention"; therefore, we are able to say that in Latin *episcopos* means "to superintend"; so one understands that he who loves to govern rather than to do good is not a bishop.

(9) It is an ancient institution that bishops are ordained priests of God through the imposition of hands by their predecessors. For Isaac the holy patriarch, placing his hand upon the head of Jacob, blessed him, and similarly also Jacob his sons. Also Moses, placing his hand over the head of Joshua son of Nun, gave him the spirit of virtue and leadership in the people of Israel. Thus also our Lord Jesus Christ, the fulfillment of the Law and the Prophets, blessed his apostles through the imposition of hands, as it is written in the Gospel of Luke: "Then he led them out as far as Bethany, and, lifting up his hands, he blessed them. While he was blessing them, he withdrew from them...and returned to Jerusalem with great joy" [Luke 24:50–52]. (10) And in the Acts of the Apostles, because of the command of the Holy Spirit, hands were imposed on the apostles Paul and Barnabas for the episcopacy, and thus they were sent out to evangelize [see Acts 13:2–3].

That one is made a priest from his thirtieth year is taken from the age of Christ when he began to preach. For this truly is the age when one no longer needs the things of a child but is full of perfection and robust and prepared for every exercise of discipline and teaching.

(11) That those who are chosen for the order of bishop should be married to only one woman is commanded even in the old Law, and the apostle wrote it more clearly: "[A bishop must be] married only once" [1 Tim 3:2]. The church seeks a priest for holy orders either from monogamy or from virginity. Priesthood is taken away from one who is married twice.

Furthermore, that a bishop is ordained not by one but by all the bishops of the same province is acknowledged to have been instituted on account of heresy, lest the tyrannical authority of one undertake anything against the faith of the church. Therefore a bishop is instituted by all those gathering around, or by no fewer than three being present, the others nevertheless consenting by testimony of letters.

(12) When he is consecrated, he is given the staff as his indication that he is either to rule or correct the people subject to him and support the infirmities of the sick. He is also given a ring as a sign of episcopal honor and for the sealing of secrets. For there are many things that, keeping hidden from the worldly and the less intelligent, priests establish as "under the seal"[9] lest the sacraments of God be exposed to those who are unworthy.

Now truly that worldly men should never be accepted into the ministry of the church that same apostolic authority teaches, saying: "Do not ordain anyone hastily" [1 Tim 5:22], and again: "[A bishop] must not be a recent convert, or he may be puffed up with conceit" [1 Tim 3:6], thinking himself adept not so much for the ministry of humility as for the administration of secular power, and be cast down by the condemnation of pride as was the devil through vainglory. (13) For how will the worldly man be strong enough to carry out the teaching office of the priesthood,[10] whose office he does not hold fast and whose discipline he does not recognize? Or what is he able to teach when he himself has not learned it? Now truly we often understand that many perform ordinations of such men, not choosing those whom the churches find useful, but those whom either they love or by whose acts of compliance they are seduced or for whom any of the elders have asked and, if I may say worse things, who achieve that they are ordained by gifts. I hold my tongue about the rest. Others make their sons or parents their successors, and prelates try to leave the dignity to their posterity, when not even Moses, the friend of God, was able to do this. Rather he chose Joshua from another tribe, so that we might know that dominion over the people is to be claimed not by blood but by way of life. (14) Occasionally, however, even persons of good stock are chosen for their merit, whence their people, having undergone the rule of a perverse bishop, will have known that there has been a government of merit.

However, the Law itself testifies that anyone who has been corrupted after baptism by some mortal sin[11] is not to be promoted to ordination. For in the Law, Moses ordered the priests that no spoiled animal be offered at the altar of God. Afterwards, the priests of Israel rejecting this, God reproached them through Malachi, saying: "O priests, who despise my name. You say, 'How have we despised your name?' By offering polluted food on my altar....And when you offer those that are lame or sick, is that not wrong?" [Mal 1:6–8]. Whence also in Numbers a red heifer, whose ashes are an expiation of the people, is not to be ordered to be offered at the altar of the Lord unless it has not done earthly works and has not borne the yoke of transgression, nor been hindered by the chains of sins [see Num 19:2]. (15) And what more can I bring up? If anyone who has already been placed in the episcopate or presbyterate should admit some mortal sin, let him be withdrawn: would it not be better [if someone] were found to be a sinner before ordination than if he were ordained? For that reason, since the law removes sinners from priesthood, let each one of them consider for themselves and, knowing that "the mighty shall be mightily put to the test" [Wis 6:7 (Vulgate)], withdraw themselves from it not because of the honor but because of the burden, and not go around occupying the place of others who are worthy.

For whoever would be the leader in learning and setting things up for the moral perfection of the people, it is necessary that he be holy in all things and be held reprehensible in nothing. For whoever accuses another of sin, ought himself to be a stranger to sin. (16) Otherwise, when he would be able to accuse his subjects to their face, would the accused be able immediately to throw back at him, "teach yourself beforehand what things are right, O bishop"? For that reason whoever neglects to do right things should desist from teaching right things. First he should correct himself who endeavors to admonish others to live well, so that in all things he himself might provide the model of living and stimulate all to good action by his own teaching and acting.

Also knowledge of the Scriptures is necessary for him. This is because if the life of a bishop is simply holy, how he is living is able to be useful for himself alone. On the other hand, if he is learned in teaching and speaking, he is able to instruct others also, both to teach his own people and to push back adversaries who, unless they have been refuted and convicted, are easily able to pervert the hearts of the simple.

(17) A bishop's speech ought to be pure, simple, and open, full of seriousness and honesty, full of sweetness and grace, discussing the mystery of the law, the doctrine of the faith, the virtue of continence, and the discipline of justice. He should admonish each one by diverse exhortation according to the quality of profession and ways of life; namely, he should find out in advance what he should offer to whom, when and how.

A special duty of the bishop, in preference to others, is to read the Scriptures, to peruse the canons, to imitate the examples of the saints, to apply himself to vigils, fasting, and prayers. He is to be at peace with his brothers, nor to look down upon anyone of his members, to condemn no one unless proven, to excommunicate no one unless examined.

A bishop will also excel equally both in humility and authority, so that neither through his excessive humility does he make the vices of his subordinates grow strong, nor through immoderate authority does he exercise a power of severity. Nevertheless, the more cautiously he fulfills his commissions, the more harshly he should fear he will be judged by Christ. (18) He will possess that charity surpassing all gifts, without which every virtue is nothing. For charity is the guardian of sanctity. However, the home of this guardian is humility. He will have also among all these things the excellence of chastity, so that the mind, thoroughly dedicated to the body of Christ, may be clean and pure from every stain of the flesh. Among these things it will be fitting that, with solicitous dispensation, he exhibit care for the poor, feed those who are hungry, clothe the naked, receive pilgrims, redeem captives, care for the widows and orphans, exhibit in all things vigilant care, providence, and discreet distribution. (19) In him also there ought to be hospitality so distinguished that he will receive all with goodness and charity. For if all the faithful desire to hear that Gospel passage, "I was a stranger and you welcomed me" [Matt 25:35], how much more so should the bishop, who ought to be the one who receives people of all kinds? For the lay person who receives one or two people has fulfilled the duty of hospitality, but a bishop is inhuman unless he receives all.

In the discerning of worldly affairs, however, it behooves him to judge the cause by merit and not by favor. For neither should a bishop so receive a powerful person that he sadden a poor one by acting against justice, nor steal justice from the powerful one for the poor man. (20) He should not defend the bad person or judge on behalf of holy things if they have been performed with injustice, nor rebuke and attack someone whose crime he may not have censured.

A bishop will also possess, according to the apostle [see 1 Tim 6:11], meekness, patience, sobriety, moderation, abstinence, or rather chastity, so that not only will he abstain from an impure act but also from the error of the eye and the word and the thought, so that, while he permits no vice to reign in him, he might be vigorous in begging pardon before God for the crimes of his subjects.

Whoever keeps observing these things will be both a useful minister of God and will retain a perfect priesthood.

VI. Auxiliary Bishops

(1) Auxiliary bishops, that is, vicars of the bishops, according to what the canons themselves testify, were instituted according to the example of the seventy elders as co-priests for the solicitude of the poor. These, constituted in towns and villages, govern churches committed to them, having permission to constitute lectors, subdeacons, and exorcists. However, they dare not ordain presbyters or deacons against the conscience of the bishop in whose region they are known to preside. For these are ordained by the bishop alone of the city that they adjoin.

VII. Presbyters

(1) The order of presbyters received its origin, as it has been said, from the sons of Aaron. For those who were called priests in the Old Testament, it is these who are now named presbyters, and those who were called chief priests are now called bishops. "Elders," how-

ever, is translated as "presbyters," because elders in the age of the Greeks are called *presbytes*.

To presbyters, as to bishops, the dispensation of the mysteries of God has been committed. (2) For they preside over the churches of Christ and are partners with the bishops in the confecting of the divine body and blood, similarly also in teaching the people and in the office of preaching. By reason of authority, the ordination and consecration of clerics is reserved solely to the bishop, lest, the discipline of the church being claimed by many, it might loosen the concord and generate scandals. Paul the apostle asserted that those presbyters, under the name of bishops, are truly priests when he says to Titus: "I left you behind in Crete for this reason, so that you should put in order what remained to be done, and should appoint elders in every town, as I directed you: someone who is blameless, married only once, whose children are believers, not accused of debauchery and not rebellious. For a bishop...must be blameless" [Titus 1:5–7]. By this statement he showed that presbyters also are to be classified under the name of bishops. (3) And when he wrote to Timothy about the ordination of the bishop and the deacon [see 1 Tim 3:1–13], he was totally silent about presbyters, because he included them in the name of bishops. For the presbyterate is a second and almost joined grade, as he also wrote to the Philippians "[with their] bishops and deacons" [Phil 1:1], since it is not possible that one city would have many bishops. Also in Acts, about to go to Jerusalem, he gathered the presbyters of the church and said to them among other things: "Keep watch over the flock, of which the Holy Spirit has ordained you bishop" [Acts 20:28].[12] And that such presbyters in the church have been constituted to be just like bishops, both the apostle says to Titus [see Titus 1:6], and the canons themselves testify.

(4) Presbyters are named such, however, by merit and wisdom, not by age. For Moses also was directed to choose presbyters. Whence it is also said in Proverbs: "the beauty of the aged is their gray hair" [Prov 20:29]. What is this gray hair? There is no doubt that it is wisdom, about which it is written: "the gray hair of men is discretion" [Wis 4:8]. When we read [Gen 5:27] that men from Adam up to Abraham had lived more than nine hundred years, no other person is first called presbyter, that is, elder, except Abraham, who is proven to have lived far fewer years. Therefore presbyters are named not on account of decrepit old age but on account of wisdom. And if this is so, it is a wonder why they are constituted foolish.

VIII. Deacons

(1) The order of deacons received its origin from the tribe of Levi. The Lord commanded Moses [see Num 3:5–26] that after the ordination of the priest Aaron and his sons, in turn the tribe of Levi should be ordained in the ministry of the divine cult, be consecrated to the Lord on behalf of all their firstborn, and serve on behalf of Israel in the presence of Aaron and his sons in the Dwelling of God. They should be attentive in the Temple day and night, and they should carry the ark and the tabernacle and all its vessels, and they should erect fortresses around the tabernacle, and in the moving of the tabernacle they should be taking it down and then later they should be erecting it again. (2) It was commanded that the Levite serve in the tabernacle "from twenty-five years old and upward" [Num 8:24]. The holy fathers also established this rule in the New Testament.

In the Gospel, however, the first things about them are found in the Acts of the Apostles: "The twelve called together the whole community of the disciples and said, 'It is not right that we should neglect the word of God in order to wait on tables. Therefore, friends, select from among yourselves seven men of good standing, full of the Spirit and of wisdom, whom we may appoint to this task, while we, for our part, will devote ourselves to prayer and to serving the word.' What they said pleased the whole community, and they chose Stephen, a man full of faith and the Holy Spirit, together with Philip, Prochorus, Nicanor, Timon, Parmenas, and Nicolaus, a proselyte of Antioch. They had these men stand before the apostles, who prayed and laid their hands on them. The word of God continued to spread; the number of the disciples increased greatly" [Acts 6:2–7]. (3) Precisely for this reason the apostles, or the successors of the apostles, decreed that there would be seven deacons throughout all the churches, who, in a more sublime rank than the others, would stand around the altar of Christ like columns of the altar. And this is not without some hidden meaning of the number seven. These deacons are those seven angels singing with trumpets we read about in the Apocalypse; they are the seven gold candelabra; they are the voices of the thunders [see Rev 1:12; 8:2; 10:3]. For with a clear voice in the manner of heralds, deacons admonish all, whether in praying, whether in genuflecting, whether in singing psalms, whether in listening to the readings. And, so that we may have ears to praise the Lord, deacons also evangelize.

Without these deacons, a priest has the name but he does not have the office. (4) For as in the case of the priest, consecration is of the sacrament, so in the minister, dispensation is of the sacrament. The priest is commanded to pray, the deacon to sing psalms. The priest sanctifies the offerings; the deacon dispenses the things sanctified. Also it is not permitted for the priests, on account of presumption, to take the chalice from the table of the Lord, unless it has been handed to them by the deacon. Levites place the offerings on the altar; Levites prepare the table of the Lord; Levites cover the ark of the testament. For not all see the high things of the mysteries which are covered by the Levites, lest they who ought not to see, see, and those who are not able to serve, lay hold of them.

For that reason deacons assist at the altar vested in albs, that they might have the heavenly life, and that they might approach the hosts immaculate and shiny white, as clean in body, uncorrupted in modesty. (5) For it is fitting that the Lord should have ministers like these, who are corrupted by no contagion of the flesh, but are more splendid in the excellence of chastity.

That deacons like these are to be ordained, the apostle Paul wrote most plainly to Timothy [1 Tim 3:8]. For when he had sent out word about the selection of the priests, he continually brought this up, saying that "deacons likewise" must be blameless, that is, without stain, just like the bishops; "chaste"—that is, they must be continent from sexual desire; "not double-tongued," lest they disturb those who have peace; "not indulging in much wine," because where there is drunkenness sexual desire and passions are in control; "not greedy for money," lest they be led away from the mystery of heaven by worldly gain. It is disgraceful to think more about the drive for gain than about things at hand. About this he stated: "And let them first be tested; then, if they prove themselves blameless, let them serve as deacons" [1 Tim 3:10]. Thus, like bishops, these also ought to be tested before ordination to see if they are worthy to minister.

IX. Guardians of Sacred Things[13]

(1) The guardians of the sacristy are Levites. These men were ordered to guard the tabernacle and all the vessels of the Temple. In the Law [see Num 8:25–26], after their fiftieth year these Levites were

chosen as guardians of the vessels. Thus, now undisturbed, after the conflict of the flesh had been subdued, they might serve God devotedly, equally with a clean body and mind, preferring the appearance of seriousness, lest they be lacking in deliberation, lest they abandon the faith, and lest they carry out anything intemperately.

X. SUBDEACONS

(1) Subdeacons, who among the Greeks are usually called *hypodiakones*, are found in Ezra [see Ezra 2:43] and are called there "Nathanites," that is, "slaves of the Lord" in humility. From their order was that Nathanael who in the Gospel of John, admonished by a divine betraying, merited to confess the savior. He also stood out as faithful at the first indication of divinity, the Lord proclaiming and saying: "Here is truly an Israelite in whom there is no deceit!" [John 1:47].

(2) Accordingly, these men receive the offerings from the people in the temple of the Lord, they are obedient to the offices of the Levites, and they also offer the vessels of the body and blood of Christ to the deacons at the altar.

Concerning them it certainly was pleasing to the fathers that those who touch the sacred mysteries be chaste and continent from women and free from every uncleanness of the flesh, according to what the prophet ordered them, teaching: "purify yourselves, you who carry the vessels of the LORD" [Isa 52:11].

When subdeacons are ordained, they do not receive the imposition of hands, as priests and Levites do, but only the paten and chalice from the hand of the bishop, and from the archdeacon the cup of water with the basin and the hand towel.[14]

XI. LECTORS

(1) The order of lectors received its form and beginning from the prophets. For it is the lectors who proclaim the word of God, to whom it is said: "Shout out, do not hold back! Lift up your voice like a trumpet!" [Isa 58:1]. While they are being ordained, the bishop cer-

tainly first speaks to the people about their manner of living, and then in the presence of the people he gives them the book of the chief points of the divine messages so that they will announce the word of God.

(2) However, the one who is promoted to this grade ought to be imbued with learning and with books, and adorned with the knowledge of meanings and words. Thus he may understand in the different kinds of sentences where the paragraph is to end, as well as where the meaning of the sentence should be placed, and where the last statement should be brought to a close. And being so equipped, he will possess the strength of the pronouncement so that he might make a deep impression on the minds and senses of all the people for their understanding. He will discern the types of pronouncements and express the proper senses of the statements, in a voice sometimes of indicating, sometimes of sorrow, sometime scolding, sometimes exhorting, or in others similar to these, according to the types of particular pronouncement. (3) Even more, there is in him the knowledge so that those ambiguous points of the sentences will be tended to. For there are many things in Scripture which, unless they are expressed in a proper manner, result in a contrary opinion, as in the following: "Who will bring any charge against God's elect? It is God who justifies" [Rom 8:33]. For if he speaks as if in a confirming manner, not keeping the style of its pronouncement, a great evil will arise. Thus therefore it is to be pronounced as if he had said: "Not God who justifies!" so that "No" might be heard. (4) It is necessary, therefore, that in all such cases there be the talent of knowledge, by which all things are properly and consistently proclaimed.

In addition, the lector needs to know the meaning of accents so that he might recognize on which syllable the stress should be placed. For inexpert lectors commonly err in the correct accentuation of words, and they are accustomed to begrudge those of us who seem to take notice of their lack of skill, drawing away and heartily swearing that they do not know what we are saying.

(5) Furthermore, the voice of the lector will be simple and clear and, accommodated to every kind of pronunciation, full of masculine flavor, shunning a boorish and rather unsophisticated tone, not too low nor yet too high, not sounding broken or weak and not at all feminine, and not with a movement of the body but only with the appearance of seriousness. The lector ought to pay attention to the ears and

the heart, not the eyes, lest he make it more important that we be spectators of him rather than hearers.

An ancient opinion is that lectors have had a special way of caring for their voice for the sake of proclaiming so that they might be able to be heard in a tumult. Thus, lectors were formerly called announcers or proclaimers.

XII. Psalmists

(1) David or Asaph stood forth as leaders or originators of psalmists, that is, of cantors [see 2 Chr 5:12]. For, after Moses, these were the first to compose and sing psalms. After Asaph died, however, his sons were proposed as substitutes in this order by David. They were psalmists through the succession of the family just as the priestly order, and these alone were singing for continual days in the temple, clothed in white stoles, the chorus responding in a single voice. (2) From this ancient custom the church took up the example of fostering psalmists by whose chanting the minds of the hearers were stirred up to the affection of God.

It behooves the psalmist to be very clear and illustrious in voice and skill, so that he may incite the souls of the hearers by the delight of sweetness. His voice will not be harsh or raucous or dissonant, but melodious, sweet, liquid, and sharp. It will have a sound and melody fitting for sacred religion, not one that exclaims a tragic style but one that demonstrates a Christian simplicity in its modulation, nor one that is redolent of musical gesture or a theatrical style but one that produces greater compunction in the hearers.

(3) The ancients abstained from food on the day before chanting. They conscientiously used yellowish green vegetables for the sake of their voice. Consequently cantors were called "beans" among the gentiles. The ancients, singing songs under plates that had been placed on the chest, demonstrated their purpose, singing with swelling voices.

Psalmists, who have been established as skilled in the art of singing, are usually chosen for this office, even without the knowledge of the bishop, solely by the decision of the presbyter.

XIII. Exorcists

(1) There are exorcists in the order and ministry of the church following the offices that were set up in the temple of Solomon and that afterwards were stationed there by the most holy Ezra. We discover that those whom Ezra recalls as agents of the Temple are now those who are the exorcists in the church of God. For the agents of the Temple under Ezra were the sons of the servants of Solomon who had the work of the Temple totally under their care, and they not only ministered to the offices of the priests but also devotedly served the sacred offerings. (2) And since they had been of the order and ministry of the Temple, they were far from the office of the altar of God, because it was not permitted for the psalmists or the porters or the servants of the sacred things to touch the gifts of the altar, except only the Levites. And why was this? The agents of the Temple had no other care except that of keeping the roofs in good order so that whatever in the building of the Temple had become shaken or fallen down, would be tended to and repaired through these agents from the treasury of the Lord. (3) Therefore the agents of the temple are exorcists among the people of God. For just as the prudent and good agent knows what the property of his master and all the manner of his substance is, and throws down before him the original records of his entire property, so also the exorcist in his diligence totally recalls the secrets of the kingdom of the Lord so that he might entrust to memory from the sacraments of the Scriptures, whence he exercises the gift that has been given to him by the Holy Spirit according to the proclamation of the apostle. (4) For the apostle had the exorcists in mind when he said: "Do all possess gifts of healing?" [1 Cor 12:30].

For when the exorcists are ordained, as the canon says, they receive from the hand of the bishop the book in which the exorcisms are written, receiving the power of placing hands upon those possessed by the devil or the catechumens.

XV (XIV).[15] Porters

(1) The porters are those who in the Old Testament are called the doormen of the Temple. They were in charge of the gates of

Jerusalem, and, assigned through their turns, guarded all the interiors and exteriors of the Temple.

These doormen, discerning between the holy and the wicked one, receive in the church only those who are faithful. Thus we cannot enter the Temple except through them. They have the power of receiving the good ones and rejecting the unworthy.

XVI (XV). MONKS

From whom did the pursuit of poverty flow down to monks? Or who stands forth as the originator of this way of living; whose style do they imitate? To the extent that it reaches to the authority of the Old Testament, I say, the leader Elijah and his disciple Elisha have been proposed, or the sons of the prophets who were living in solitude and, having left the cities, were making for themselves little houses near the Jordan River. It has also been proposed, in the Gospel [see Matt 3:4], that John the Baptist stands forth as the originator, who lived alone in the desert, fed only by locusts and wild honey. Now, since that time, the originators of this way of life are the most noble leaders, Paul, Anthony, Hilary, Macarius, and the other fathers. From their examples the holy institution of monks has been kindled throughout the world.

(2) There are six categories of monks, of which three are the best; the remaining are truly detrimental and to be avoided in all cases.

The first category is that of the cenobites, that is, of those living in common, following the example of those saints who at the time of the apostles in Jerusalem, having sold and distributed all their belongings to the poor, were living in holy communion of life, not saying that anything was theirs alone, "but everything they owned was held in common" [Acts 4:32]. They were one mind and one heart in God. These therefore are taken to be the beginning of the institution of the monastery.

(3) The second category is that of the hermits who, receding far from men, are reported to seek out and live in desert places and vast wildernesses, in imitation of Elijah and John the Baptist, who entered isolated places of the desert. Since they have an incredible contempt for the world, they are attracted to solitude alone, eating only wild

plants, or they are content with bread and water alone, which is given to them for certain intervals of time. Thus, deep in most removed places and far from every sight of men, they are delighted only by divine conversation to which they have clung with pure minds and for love of which they have left behind not only the world but also human contact.

(4) The third category is that of the anchorites, who, already perfected by a cenobitic way of life, shut themselves up in little cells removed far from the sight of men, allowing no access to themselves but living only in contemplation of God.

(5) The fourth category is that of those who flatter themselves with the image of anchorites. These, as Cassian says,[16] in their beginnings seem to seek the perfection of the *coenobium* with a certain brief fervor; but, immediately made lukewarm, they withdraw from cutting back on their earlier customs and vices. They are not content to sustain any longer the yoke of humility and patience, and they scorn being placed under the rule of the elders. They desire separate cells and they seek to sit alone so that, challenged by no one, they might be esteemed mild and humble. This arrangement, or rather, lukewarmness, never permits those, once it has infected them, to reach perfection. (6) In this fashion, not only are their vices not truly cut off, but, even worse, they regain their strength while being provoked by no one, so that like some lethal and internal virus, spreading ever more profoundly the more it is hidden, it generates an incurable disease in the sick man. For out of reverence of the cell of the individual no one now dares to rebuke the vices of the solitary one, of which he preferred to be ignorant rather than be cured.

(7) The fifth category is that of the wanderers,[17] who under the garb of monks wander here and there, spreading around hypocrisy for sale, traveling around the provinces, never sent, never attached, never standing, never sitting. Some make up things that they have not seen, having their own opinions on behalf of God. Some sell parts of the bodies[18] of martyrs, if they are martyrs. Some magnify their fringes and phylacteries [see Matt 23:5], chasing after glory from men. Some walk about long-haired, lest sanctity be thought of more cheaply tonsured than long-haired, so that of course whoever sees them will think of those ancients whom we read about, like Samuel and Elijah and others. (8) Some assert that they themselves have honors that they have not received. Some lie that their parents

and siblings have dared themselves to live in this or that region and they are traveling to them. All of them beg, all of them demand either the expense of monetary need or the value of simulated sanctity. In the meantime, wherever they are discovered in their bad deeds or words, or become notorious in any way, the thing done is reviled under the name of monks in general.

(9) The sixth category of monks is itself the worst and neglected one that sprouted at the origin of the church through Ananias and Sapphira and was cut down by the severity of the apostle Peter [see Acts 5:1–11]. From the fact that they themselves withdraw from the cenobitic discipline and follow their own free wills, these are called in the language of the Egyptians *sarabaitae*[19] or those who refuse.[20] They construct cells for themselves and call them by the false name of monasteries. Free from the rule of the elders, they live by their own desire, laboring in works certainly not to distribute them to the poor but to acquire monies which they hoard. As Jerome says about them,[21] as a work of art may be holy but not the life [of the artist], whatever they sell is more expensive. (10) In truth, as Jerome also says, they usually contend in fasting, and they make this thing of secrecy a thing of victory. Among them all things are affected, he says, loose sleeves, flapping boots, thicker clothing, frequent sighs, visitation of virgins, detraction of clerics, and whenever a feast day comes they fill themselves until they vomit.

(11) Cassian distinguishes between a *coenobium* and a monastery in this way: the habitation of even only one monk can be called a monastery, but not a *coenobium*, unless it is the dwelling place of many.[22]

I will talk briefly about the way of life of monks as the style of the fathers teaches. Monks certainly, as it has been said above, first having held in contempt and having deserted the allurements of this world, live a most holy life, having gathered in common, living in prayers, in readings, in disputations, in vigils, in fasting. Inflated by no pride, jealous with no envy, but modest in a calm sense of reverence, they follow a most harmonious life, and revealing their thoughts to one another, they discuss among themselves, they smooth things out. (12) No one possesses anything earthly as his own lot. They do not wear precious or colorful clothing, but the most common and practical. They use baths never for the pleasure of the body, but rarely, on account of the necessity of listlessness. They never proceed without consulting the

abbot, nor is anything taken up by them without the will of the pater-
nal consent. They work with their hands at those things that can support their body without being able to distract their mind from God.
They chant, working by their hands, and they are consoled in this
work as by a divine shout or rhythmic call.[23] (13) They hand over their
work to those whom they call deans because these are set over groups
of ten, so that the care of their body might concern none of them
either in food or in clothing or whatever other work there is either of
daily necessity or, as is usual, of changed importance. The deans hand
over these things to the prior. The prior, however, disposing of all
things with great solicitude, makes to be at hand whatever their life
demands because of the weakness of the body. Nevertheless he also
provides an explanation to the one they call "father."[24] These fathers,
noted for toleration of intellect and discretion, excelling in all things
without pride, look after those they call sons. Their own authority is
great in ordering; the willingness of these others is great in obeying.
(14) Frequently, the sign being given, they all gather by night and by
day with swift haste to the prayer of the solemn hours, celebrating
with fixed intention of heart and persisting all the way to the end of
the psalms without weariness. In the same way they gather, some days
intervening, while they are still fasting, in a conference in order to
hear the father. They listen to him, however, with incredible zeal, in
great silence and signifying either by sighing or by tears the emotions
of their souls, insofar as the discourse of the one discussing shall have
challenged them. They feed the body in the "great silence" only as
much as is necessary that they may be healthy. Each one restrains
through parsimony the appetite of concupiscence lest their heart be
weighed down, perhaps, with those paltry and most worthless things
that are at hand. (15) Therefore they abstain not only from meats and
from wine as is necessary, so that the libido may be subdued, but also
from all things that provoke the appetite of the stomach and the
mouth. Certainly, whatever food is left over, necessarily so owing to
the works of the hands and the restriction of the food served, is distributed with great care to the needy so that nothing remains that
might be in abundance.

To the purpose of this sacred army come not only free men but
also many from the condition of slavery, or who on account of which
have been freed by their masters or, preferably, are about to be freed.
(16) They come also from a rustic life and from training in the crafts

and from common labor, certainly more happily to the extent they are more strongly educated. If these are not admitted, it is a grave crime. For many of this number stood out and are greatly to be imitated. For on that account "God chose what is foolish in the world to shame the wise; God chose what is weak in the world to shame the strong; God chose what is low and despised in the world, things that are not, to reduce to nothing things that are, so that no one might boast in the presence of God" [1 Cor 1:27–29].

(17) In similar fashion there are also *coenobia* of women who are solicitously and chastely serving God. These, segregated in their little dwellings and remote from the men as far away as possible, are nevertheless joined to them in devoted love of sanctity and pursuit of virtue. No young man has access to them, nor any of the old men, even if they are most serious and proven, except up to the vestibule, for the purpose of bringing necessary things that they lack. Individual women who are most serious and proven are placed in charge of these *coenobia*, expert and prepared not only in instituting and ordering manners of living but also in teaching minds. By weaving they also exercise and sustain the body, and they provide this clothing to the monks who are men, bringing back from each of them whatever their means of providing their living is.

Coenobia of virgins and monks seem to maintain these customs, this life, this institution.

(18) Monks are chosen according to humility. To be sure, the disease of vainglory stains many of them, and abstinence puffs up many, and knowledge exalts. They do good things, but for fame and not for eternal life, in other words so that they may grasp the glory of praise or reach the height of the desired honor. Among them discord often arises, and the jealousy of envy concerning fraternal successes is produced, the love of temporal things walks about, pursuing earthly yearnings just as uselessly as frequently, doing so before human eyes without shame. Such as these, therefore, should never be called monks, because they are joined to God only by profession and not by action.

XVII (XVI). PENITENTS

(1) Job first showed forth the example for penitents, when, after funerals or scourges, still in his refuting and also in haircloth and

ashes he lifted up laments of repentance saying: "Therefore...I repent in dust and ashes" [Job 42:6]. After him David gave us an instruction on repentance when, fallen with a grave wound, he heard his sin from the prophet. He repented immediately and healed his wound with the confession of penance. (2) Thus the people of Nineveh and many others confessed their sins and carried out their penance. The kinds of things they had done were displeasing to God, and the kinds of things they did through God were pleasing to him.

Penance is the medicine for the wound, the hope of salvation, through which sinners are saved, through which God is moved to mercy. Penance is not weighed in time but by the profundity of sorrow and tears. The name penance is taken from the pain by which the soul is tormented and the flesh is mortified.

(3) These truly who carry out penance accordingly grow their hair and beard, so that they may demonstrate the abundance of the crimes by which the head of the sinner is weighed down. For hairs are accepted for vices, as it is written: "The iniquities of the wicked ensnare them, and they are caught in the toils of their sin" [Prov 5:22]. "And," as the apostle says, "Does not nature itself teach you that if a man wears long hair, it is degrading to him?" [1 Cor 11:14]. Therefore penitents accept this ignominy because of their sins.

(4) Truly because they are prostrate in haircloth, through the haircloth there is remembrance of the sins because the goats will be on the left hand in the future times. Therefore confessing we are prostrate in haircloth, saying, "and my sin is ever before me" [Ps 50(51):5]. They are sprinkled with ashes, either so that they are reminded that they are ash and dust or because they have been made dust; that is, they were made wicked. Thus even those liars, the first humans, drawing away from God and, having done evil things, injuring the creature, returned in ashes, having put them on. Therefore it is good that the penitent deplores his sin in haircloth and ashes, because in the haircloth is the roughness and the pricking of sins, and in the ashes is shown the dust of those who have died. (5) Because of that we do penance in either way so that both in the pricking of the haircloth we might know the vices that we committed through our fault, and through the "spark of the ash" we may ponder the sentence of death to which we arrive by sinning.

The Catholic Church faithfully imposes the practicing of the remedy of penance in the hope of merciful forgiveness. After the one sacrament of baptism, which, commended by singular tradition, it solicitously prohibits from being repeated, it proposes the help of penance as a medicinal remedy. (6) Everyone ought to know that they are in need of this remedy for the daily excesses of human fragility without which it is not possible to be in this life. (Strictly speaking, in order to protect the dignity of their positions, only God can serve as a witness of this for priests and deacons; for all others truly a priest solemnly testifies to this before God.) Thus, in this life a fruitful confession covers what the rash appetite or the neglect of ignorance is seen to have brought about. Thus, as we believe that in baptism all sins are remitted or through martyrdom sin is imputed to no one, so also by the fruitful compunction of penance we acknowledge that all sins are removed. Thus, the tears of penitents are calculated before God the same as baptism. Thus, even if the sins are great, or even if they are grave, there is nothing in them that requires us to despair of the mercy of God.

(7) However, in the doing of penance, as it has been said above, the measure of time is not to be considered as much as the measure of sorrow. For "a broken and contrite heart, O God, you will not despise" [Ps 50(51):19]. Nevertheless, as much intention of the rash mind toward evil as there was in sinning, it is necessary that there be as much investment in lamentation. For the sorrow of the penitent is twofold: one when we lament what we have done wrong, the second when we do not do what we ought to be doing. For that person truly does penance who does not neglect to do penance for past deeds and does not commit anything that would still need to be repented of. The one who truly pours out tears unceasingly and nevertheless does not stop sinning, this one has the lament but does not have the cleansing.

(8) If, however, through the grace of God they have been converted to penitence, they should not be disturbed if once again, after their correction, the abandoned vices knock at the heart. These vices are not able to harm a good way of life if such a thought does not break out in agreement or action. For to endure the thoughts of vices without carrying them out is not for damnation but for probation; it is not the occasion of undergoing separation but rather of increasing virtue.

For if anyone near the end of his life stops being evil through penitence, he ought not therefore despair because he is at the end of a terrible life, because God does not look at how we have been before but how we are at the end of life. (9) For from his end each one is either justified or condemned, as it is written: "The LORD will judge the ends of the earth" [1 Sam 2:10] and elsewhere, "For he looks to the ends of the earth" [Job 28:24]. Therefore we are not in doubt about the end of the man justified through the sorrow of penitence. Nevertheless, since it ought to be done rarely, it is to be feared that if the hoped-for conversion is deferred until the end, death will seize us before penitence comes to our assistance. For this reason, even if conversion is good at the last moment, nevertheless it is better that it occur long before the end so that the transition from this life might be more secure.

XVIII (XVII). VIRGINS

(1) Now however, I will briefly discuss what is the soundness of sacred virginity or from whom the pursuit of such a sacred proposition has arisen. For to the extent that it pertains to the Old Testament, Elijah, Jeremiah, and Daniel are recognized as the first to have pursued the good of chastity and continence. To the extent that it pertains to the New Testament, Christ is the head of the male virgins; Mary is the head of the female virgins. She is their author; she is the mother of our head, who is both son of a virgin and bridegroom of virgins. Hence masses of men and holy young women, male and female followers of perpetual continence, have sprouted, chastising themselves not only in body but also castrating themselves in the very root of concupiscence, pondering the heavenly and angelic life in earthly mortality and holding perpetual incorruptibility in corruptible flesh. By these is given up all fecundity of the flesh, all conjugal chastity. (2) For since this universal church "as a chaste virgin" is "promised in marriage to one husband" [2 Cor 11:2], how much more worthy of honor are its members who preserve even in their own flesh what the whole church preserves in faith?

But even if virginity is so praised, marriage is not condemned. It is fitting, therefore, not to condemn what is good but to recommend what is better. For before the arrival of Christ, of course, marriages were pleasing to God; after the advent of Christ, virginity. The first statement of God commanded us to grow and generate; the second recommended continence. Now is not the place of his voice: "Be fruitful and multiply" [Gen 1:22, 28; 9:1, 7; 35:11]; for now the other voice has superseded: "Woe to those who are pregnant and to those who are nursing infants in those days!" [Luke 21:23], and again: "the appointed time has grown short; from now on, let even those who have wives be as though they had none" [1 Cor 7:29]. (3) Nevertheless, unless I am mistaken, both are the proclamation of one and the same God. Then, in the beginning, God certainly sent forth the sowing of the people, giving free rein to marriage until the world was filled up. Now truly, under the most extreme of times, he has restrained what he had let loose and he has revoked what he had granted. Thus Solomon, prophesying in the Spirit, said: "a time to embrace, and a time to refrain from embracing" [Eccl 3:5]. It is of the Old Precept that the earth be filled with those who are procreating; it is of the New, however, that the heavens be filled by continence and virginity.

Nevertheless, it remains unchanged that virginity is of lofty and sublime reward, for when in some place the apostles said: "If such is the case of a man with his wife, it is better not to marry" [Matt 19:10], the Lord responded to them: "Let anyone accept this who can" [Matt 19:12]. (4) Thus, there is no precept concerning those who are continent, but there is a recommendation. Virginity is not embraced as if out of necessity, but as voluntary so that it is able to be praised. So the apostle asserts: "Now concerning virgins, I have no command of the Lord, but I give my opinion as one who by the Lord's mercy is trustworthy. I think that, in view of the impending crisis, it is well for you to remain as you are" [1 Cor 7:25–26]. But truly it is necessary that those who cannot bear the temptation of the flesh must knock at the door of marriage. Whence the same apostle says: "But if they are not practicing self-control, they should marry. For it is better to marry than to be aflame with passion" [1 Cor 7:9]; and again: "But if you marry, you do not sin, and if a virgin marries, she does not sin" [1 Cor 7:28]. Since you are of free will, if there is not the ability to be the greater, then be the lesser. (5) Marriage is not a sin, but those who marry out of solicitude for the world are barely able to keep the law of God.

In addition, he says that they who have not yet vowed themselves to God in chastity do not sin if they marry. But the one who has promised in his heart, if he does otherwise, as the same apostle says: "and so they incur condemnation for having violated their first pledge" [1 Tim 5:12]. For what was lawful through nature, he made unlawful for himself through a vow, just as it was in no way lawful that Ananias and

Sapphira retain anything from the worth of their possessions; on account of which they were struck down by instant death.

(6) In the Gospel diverse categories of virgins are mentioned. But the possession of the kingdom is especially assigned to those who castrate themselves out of love of God, that is, not those whom the necessity of impossibility forces, but those whom the will makes continent. For so it is written, as the Lord affirms: "For there are eunuchs who have been so from birth, and there are eunuchs who have been made eunuchs by others, and there are eunuchs who have made themselves eunuchs for the sake of the kingdom of heaven" [Matt 19:12]. To these he also speaks through Isaiah the prophet, saying that he "will give, in my house and within my walls, a monument and a name better than sons and daughters" [Isa 56:5]. (7) But for those who are born this way or for whom that virile member is disabled so that they are not able to generate, since they are eunuchs in potency and in exercise, it suffices that they become Christians and keep the precepts of God. Nevertheless, it being the situation that they would have married if they had been able, they are put on the same level, therefore, as the other faithful married ones in the household of God. This is because they are castrated because of the world, not because of the kingdom of heaven. They do not take wives by virtue of the spirit but by necessity of the flesh.

(8) However, to demonstrate how great a gift of sanctity there is in virgins, John also ordered only those "who have not defiled themselves with women" [Rev 14:4] to cling to the feet of the Lamb. These are the hundred and forty-four thousand of the saints playing on their harps, of unimpaired virginity in their body, of inviolate chastity in their heart, "who follow the Lamb wherever he goes" [Rev 14:4], whom no one either dares or is worthy to follow except only the virginal one. Therefore the rest of the faithful who have lost the virginity of the body also follow the Lamb, but not wherever he goes, but only as far as they are able. (9) Thus it is to be feared that so great a gift of sanctity not be corrupted by pride. For virginity extols many; continence elevates. For I say faithfully, humble married people follow the Lamb more easily than proud virgins, even if not wherever he goes, certainly as far as they are able. For how does one follow after the one whom one does not want to reach? Or how does one reach the person who does not come as one who has learned "that I am gentle and humble in heart"? [Matt 11:29]. Therefore virgins continue

on the road of sublimity by the footstep of humility. They follow Christ by holding with perseverance to that which they vowed ardently, so that they correspond also in other actions of professed and guarded integrity, without which undoubtedly virginity remains useless and empty. For good actions, if they are added to virginity, exhibit the angelic life to humans and the ways of heaven to the earth.

(10) Therefore those virgins are to be commended who are devoted to continence in such a way that they are weighed down by no crimes and by no burden of earthly solicitude. For marital union begets care of the world, as Paul teaches when he says: "I want you to be free from anxieties. The unmarried man is anxious about the affairs of the Lord, how to please the Lord; but the married man is anxious about the affairs of the world, how to please his wife" [1 Cor 7:32–33]. Whence it is recognized that a vow of continence of this kind is not able to please God because it is hindered by the impediment of worldly cares. For it profits nothing that those who are hampered by worldly cares be detached from the action of the flesh, except only that they acquire for themselves greater supplications for it because they by no means conquer the world who were able to conquer the flesh.

(11) It is asked, however, why female virgins are veiled for their consecration. This is the reason for it. Women are not at all ordered in ecclesiastical rankings or offices. For it is not permitted for them to speak or teach in the church [see 1 Cor 14:34; 1 Tim 2:12], and they may not baptize nor offer nor appropriate for themselves a share in any masculine gift or priestly office. Therefore in this case only, because she is a virgin and has proposed to sanctify her flesh, because of that let the indulgence of a veil be extended to her that she may enter the church as a notable or decorated person and show the honor of the sanctified body in the freedom of the head, and wear the miter as a crown of virginal glory on the top of her head.

XIX (XVIII). Widows

(1) There are many examples of widows, of whom the first one who is read about in the Scriptures is Naomi. It is read that a widow was sent to Elijah. It is written also that the Shunammite widow was supposed to receive Elisha and give him food. There is also that

admirable widow Judith, who triumphed over Holofernes, the leader of the Assyrians, and brought back her purity intact, having conquered the man who was her host. Moreover, in the New Testament Anna is the first widow read about, who recognized the Lord as an infant, who merited to recognize the grace of his divinity before she was able to hear his word.

(2) The rank of widow is almost joined to virginity. Thus it was a widow who first recognized Christ, whom a virgin bore. Therefore the virgin is joyful because she is intact, the widow even more so because she is expert. Nevertheless, the reward of both is with the Lord, first the virgin, then the other.

The apostle calls that one a widow who, after the ending of one marriage, from that point on renounces sex. He says: "Let a widow be put on the list if she is not less than sixty years old and has been married only once" [1 Tim 5:9]. Whence the consequence is that a woman who has been joined in several marriages lacks the name of widow.

(3) The same apostle carefully describes the kind of persons widows ought to be [1 Tim 5:10], saying: "She must be well attested for her good works," as was the case with Tabitha. If she "has brought up children," she is heard by God. She will have "shown hospitality, washed the saints' feet, helped the afflicted"—that is, the sick or those placed in prison—"and devoted herself to doing good in every way." Thus Paul briefly concludes this entire section indicating that in all things widows should be models of how to live. And again Paul writes to Titus: "Tell the older women to be reverent in behavior" [Titus 2:3], so that widows should be like these holy ones in their walking and movements, appearances, speech, and silence, and so that they prefer the dignity of sacred continence. (4) After this he adds that they are "not to be slanderers or slaves to drink" [Titus 2:3], but using little; for women of these ages, whose pleasures of the body have grown cold, are accustomed to giving themselves wine for their libido. After this he adds that "they are to teach what is good, so that they may encourage the young women to love their husbands [and] to love their children" [Titus 2:3–4]. Certainly it is permitted to them to teach, but only women and this not in church but privately. For this category of common women is accustomed to be talkative. Whence the same apostle notes that certain of the widows are inquisitive and verbose, and he says that this vice comes from idleness. "Besides, they

learn to be idle, gadding about from house to house," since they have no fear of being detained or of being subjected to the power of the husband, "and they are not merely idle, but also gossips and busybodies, saying what they should not say" [1 Tim 5:13].

(5) This apostle predicts that widows who desire marriage after a resolution of continence will have damnation: "for when their sensual desires alienate them from Christ, they want to marry, and so they incur condemnation for having violated their first pledge" [1 Tim 5:11–12], that is, because they did not stand firm in that which they first vowed. Nevertheless he does not say "they marry" but "they want to marry." It is not the love of a very distinguished resolution that calls many of them away from marrying, but rather the fear of obvious disgrace. (6) Therefore there are those who wish to marry and yet do not marry because they are not able to do so with impunity—for it is better that they not vow and marry than to be burned, that is, than to be destroyed by the hidden flame of concupiscence! There are those who repent of the profession and are irked by the confession. These, unless they direct their heart correctly and in turn conquer the libido by fear of God, are to be reckoned among the dead, whether they occupy themselves in pleasures (whence the apostle says: "the widow who lives for pleasure is dead even while she lives" [1 Tim 5:6]), or whether [they occupy themselves] by serving in works and fasting with no correction of their heart, and with more ostentation than emendation.

XX (XIX). MARRIED PEOPLE

(1) The law of nature concerning married people is of the world. For God made Adam and gave him Eve as a helper with the subsequent intention of procreation, saying: "Be fruitful and multiply, and fill the earth" [Gen 1:22, 28; 9:1, 7; 35:11]. But, having been created, the woman was first a comfort rather than a wife, until God drove out of paradise for disobedience those whom he had brought into paradise for obedience. After his departure from the blessed home, the one expelled came to know his wife as the Book of Genesis teaches: "Now the man knew his wife Eve, and she conceived and bore a son" [Gen 4:1]. (2) Therefore the married couple proceeded to the assigned work, and enduring "thorns and thistles" [Gen 3:18], went

about fulfilling the task God had first assigned. Weariness followed in procreating. For this reason an edict of this kind about childbearing had come first: "In pain shall you bring forth children" [Gen 3:16], so that we might understand that those creatures who had turned away in such fashion had stolen away in misfortunes and grief. Whence the apostle predicted, saying: "those who marry will experience distress in this life" [1 Cor 7:28].

Nevertheless, the beds of the married are not dishonorable [see Heb 13:4], nor is the marriage bed that is without fruit immaculate. For there are offspring of saints, and what is praised in virginity is a product of marriage; therefore neither do we say that marriage is sinful, nor nevertheless do we equate it to the virginal goodness of continence or even that of the widow. (3) Thus, marriages are good in themselves. They become bad through those things that are done around them. For they are bad through those things about which the apostle speaks: "but the married man is anxious about the affairs of the world, how to please his wife" [1 Cor 7:33], and again, "because of cases of sexual immorality, each man should have his own wife" [1 Cor 7:2].

However, this first union, having been made in a divine manner, serves as a model that not one man and many women, but one man and one woman are to be married. For when God had shaped man and had seen ahead of time that a partner was necessary for him, having obtained one from his rib, he formed one woman for him. Thus Adam and his wife Eve, engaged in one marital union between themselves, sanctified the pattern for men by the authority of their origin and the primal will of God. So, in accordance with spiritual marriages, as the one Christ and the one church, so also [there is to be only] one man and one wife, both as according to the pattern of the human race and as according to the sacrament of Christ. (4) Having a number of marriage partners, however, began from a sinful man; first Lamech, having married two women [Gen 4:19], made three in one flesh. But you respond that even the patriarchs were using several wives at the same time; therefore, on account of this it will be lawful for us to take several. Reasonably it will be allowed, if these prefigurements of some future sacrament survive, by which many marriage partners are symbolized.

However, the apostle orders second marriages on account of incontinence. "For it is better" for one man once again "to marry" [1 Cor 7:9] than because of an expanded libido to fornicate with very many. More often now, however, the license for marrying is not from religion but from sin.

(5) That married people are blessed by a priest in this coming together, is explained by the fact that this was done by God in the first condition of men. For thus it is written: "So God created humankind in his image, in the image of God he created them; male and female he created them. God blessed them, and God said to them, 'Be fruitful and multiply'" [Gen 1:27–28]. Therefore in this likeness there is done now in the church what was done then in paradise.

The custom is that bridesmaids with only one husband are utilized by virgins themselves who are legitimately marrying. Naturally this is on account of monogamy and, even if [it is done] because of an omen, nevertheless it is a good omen.

(6) Truly these women, when they are married, are veiled, so that they will know always to be subject to their husbands and humble. They call this veiling "bad luck"[25] in popular speech, that is, "of Mars,"[26] because the sign of marital dignity and power is in the man, for "the husband is the head of his wife" [1 Cor 11:3]. This practice is allowed, and consequently they are veiled when they marry, so that they may know the modesty of womanhood, because now it follows that from then on she is modest. Thus it was with Rebekah, who, when she was being taken to her spouse, at the same time as she saw him, did not wait for a greeting or a kiss, but immediately thinking what was to come, veiled her head with a cover. From this also are the wives' tales that they should veil their heads; for it is said to veil and to cover up. Thus also clouds are called such by the fact that they cover the heavens.

(7) After the blessing by the deacon, those being married are joined by a cord, one to the other, lest they disrupt the joining together of conjugal unity. This binding is of a mixed white and purple color. The white is for the cleanliness of life; the purple is used for the posterity of blood, so that by this sign is meant that the law of continence will be kept by both until the time it is suggested, and also that after this the obligation to be paid will not be denied. The apostle says this to the married: abstain yourselves "for a time to devote yourselves to prayer"—this the white of the cord implies; but he adds: "then come together again" [1 Cor 7:5]—the color purple demonstrates this.

(8) This is the reason that first of all a ring is given by the husband to his wife; this is done certainly either as a sign of mutual faithfulness, or even better, that their hearts may be joined by this pledge.

Consequently, the ring is placed on the fourth finger so that by the vein in it something of the blood, as it is carried, will arrive all the way to the heart. In former times, however, nothing more was given by one, lest the plurality [of signs] divide the one love.

In the house of Israel, however, it was unlawful that a girl be given to a man unless it was after maturity had been manifested by blood [Deut 22:13–21].

(9) In choosing husbands, among the ancients these four things were looked at: virtue, family, attractiveness, and habit of prayer; in women, three things: if she was generous, if she was well-mannered, if she was beautiful. Now, however, neither the family nor the customs, but rather riches are pleasing among women. Nor is the woman asked if she is chaste, but rather how shapely, which both feeds the libido of concupiscence and draws the deep breaths of all after it. For a beautiful woman, as some wise man said,[27] is quickly fallen in love with and the one whom many love is guarded with difficulty.

There are, however, arranged marriages that require in the union not pleasure but offspring. For these unions are established not so that they serve the pleasures of the flesh, but only to seek the fruit of propagation. (10) For even as their dowry stipulations indicate, the wife is taken "for the sake of procreating children."[28] When, therefore, anyone lives more pleasurably than the necessity of procreating children demands, immediately it is a sin. Whence it is necessary that by daily alms and prayers they intercede who by frequent use stain the purity of their conjugal bed through incontinence.

The goods of marriage are three: offspring, fidelity, and sacrament. With regard to fidelity, it is attended to unless contrary to the conjugal bond the marriage partner sleeps together with another woman or another man; with regard to offspring, that the child be received lovingly and nourished purely; with regard to sacrament, that the bond not be broken nor that one be married to another for the sake of offspring.

(11) Therefore it is said to be a sacrament between married people because, as it is not possible that the church be divided from Christ, neither can a wife from the man. What is the case, therefore, in Christ and in the church, is thereby an inseparable sacrament of union in the individuals who are men and wives. Consequently the apostle says: "To the married I give this command—not I but the Lord—that the wife should not separate from her husband" [1 Cor 7:10]. It is pro-

hibited to be sent away for whatever reason, in order that they not be married to others according to the custom of the Jews that the Lord forbade, saying: "whoever divorces his wife, except for unchastity, and marries another commits adultery" [Matt 19:9]. Only that is adultery, as Jerome says,[29] which conquers the affection of the wife. Indeed, when she shall have divided one flesh into two and shall have separated herself by fornication, she ought not to be retained by the husband, lest it make the man be also under a curse, as Scripture says: "But he who keeps an adulteress is a fool and wicked" [Prov 18:22 (Vulgate)]. Wherever there is fornication and the suspicion of fornication, the wife is freely sent away. (12) What therefore? If she is sterile, if deformed, if in poor old age, if stinking, if intoxicated, if irritable, if bad in morals, if luxurious, if foolish, if gluttonous, if wandering, if a quarrelsome person and abusive, it must be that she will be kept, veils not wanting, and whoever else of this kind has been accepted is to be retained. For when you were free, you subjected yourself to slavery freely. But whoever has a wife, as Lactantius says,[30] will be able to have neither a slave nor a free woman in order to preserve the faithfulness of the marriage. For, as is the reasoning of public law, neither is only the wife an adulterer, who, having a husband, is polluted by another, while the husband, if he should have another woman, is held free from the crime of adultery, since divine law has joined the two into one body of matrimony [see Matt 19:4–6], so that whoever breaks the union of the body into different parts is an adulterer. Therefore the faithfulness is to be kept by one and the other. (13) In fact, the wife is to be taught by the example of continence of the husband, so that she may conduct herself chastely. For it is evil that you do that which you are not able to grant; for the man is head of the wife [Eph 5:23]. When the woman lives better than the man, however, the house hangs down from the top. Therefore the man ought to surpass his wife in all good things, for he is the head, so that she may imitate the man and truly follow, as the body follows its head, just as the church follows Christ.

The apostle encourages that the married also abstain for the sake of prayer, and "by agreement" observe times of sanctification, and without carnal impediment "devote yourselves to prayer" [1 Cor 7:5]. For also in the Old Testament before they were sanctified all the men abstained from women and thus they merited to attend God coming down onto the mountain.

(14) Again the same apostle encourages, "Wives, be subject to your husbands" [Col 3:18]. For many, blown away by riches and nobility against their simpler men, do not remember the teaching of God by which they are subject to them. Indeed the Lord said to the woman: "your desire shall be for your husband and he shall rule over you" [Gen 3:16]. Therefore the precepts of Sacred Scripture are to be obeyed, and the man is to be served by a free servitude and a full affection. For the man was not created for the woman but the woman for the man; and since "the head of a woman is her husband," but "Christ is the head of every man" [1 Cor 11:3], whichever wife is not subject to her husband, that is, to her head, does a crime of the same sort as that of her husband if he is not subject to Christ, his head. (15) The word of the Lord is blasphemed both when the first teaching of God is held in disrepute and it is accounted as nothing, and the Gospel of Christ is dishonored when, contrary to the law of nature and the faith, she who is Christian and subject to the law of God desires to be superior to the man. Even pagan women serve their husbands by the common law of nature. Therefore the law of nature and of God is served, if the woman is subject to the husband. But on the contrary, if she desires to rule her husband, both the order of nature is overturned and that house is called miserable and perverse.

XXI.

And now we will explain the procedure of the sacraments and the order of those coming to the faith. Of these the first grade is that of the catechumens, the second of the elect and the third of the baptized.

(XX). CATECHUMENS, EXORCISM, AND SALT

Catechumens are those who are first coming from paganism, having the desire to believe in Christ. Because the first precept of exhortation in the Law is: "Hear, O Israel: The LORD is our God, the LORD alone" [Deut 6:4], it is for that reason that the one to whom God first spoke through the priest, as if through Moses, is named catechumen, that is, the one hearing. Thus, knowing the one God, the person may leave various errors of false gods. (2) I think, however, that all those baptized unto repentance by John the Baptist went before as a prefiguring of the catechumens.

Catechumens are first exorcised, and then they receive grains of salt and are anointed.

The exorcism is a word of rebuke against the unclean spirit, made to those possessed by the devil or to catechumens, through which there might be driven out of them the most evil power of the devil. It can be either a long-standing evil or a violent incursion that is expelled. (3) The epileptic[31] whom "Jesus rebuked...and the demon came out of him" [Matt 17:17] was a sign of this. The power of the devil is exorcised and the catechumens are breathed upon, that they might renounce him and, freed from the power of darkness, be carried into the kingdom of the Lord himself through the sacrament of baptism. Because little children in themselves are not able to renounce, this action is fulfilled through the hearts and mouths of those carrying [them].[32]

The practice that salt is to be given in the ministry to the catechumens was instituted by the fathers, so that in their tasting of it they might perceive the condiment of wisdom and not act foolishly away from the taste of Christ. Nor are they to be foolish and look back like the wife of Lot, lest giving bad example they remain and season others, (4) just as she who, when she was liberated from Sodom, standing on the road looked back and remained there, having been made a pillar of salt. By this sign of salt the catechumens are seasoned, these who through faith renounced the world and its acts and desires, lest these former things be remembered with their original affection and so that these catechumens will not be called back to the allurements of the world. For according to the teaching of the savior, "No one who puts a hand to the plow and looks back is fit for the kingdom of God" [Luke 9:62].

XXII (XXI). THE ELECT

(1) After the catechumens, the second grade is of the elect. The elect are those who now, after the teaching of the faith, after continence of life, are rushing forward to receive the grace of Christ. Therefore they are called the elect, that is, those "seeking" the grace of Christ. For the

catechumens only hear; they do not yet seek. They are like guests and neighbors of the faithful. They hear the mysteries from outside [after being dismissed]; they hear the grace, but as of yet they are not called faithful. (2) The elect, however, already seek; they already receive; they already are catechized; that is, they are imbued with instruction about the sacraments. For to these the saving Symbol is handed over as the norm of the faith of the community and the confession of the saints, by which, having been instructed, they may know how they now ought to present themselves according to the grace of Christ.

XXIII (XXII). The Symbol [Creed]

(1) The Symbol, the very same that the elect receive, our elders said was instituted for this reason: they hand down in these words that, after the ascension of our Lord and savior to the Father, when through the advent of the Holy Spirit his inflamed disciples were speaking to all the nations in tongues (by which presentiment it follows that no people is seen as foreign to them, no barbarian tongue is inaccessible or without a way), the precept was given to them by the Lord to go out to preach the word of God to each and every nation. (2) About to depart from one another, therefore, they first established in common a norm for their future preaching, lest going away from each other to different locations, something different or dissonant might be preached to those who were being invited to faith in Christ. Therefore, all of them gathered as one and, filled with the Holy Spirit, they composed for themselves a brief rule of preaching by discussing in one body what they were thinking, and they determined that this standard was to be given to the believers.

(3) They wanted to entitle this a symbol for many and most just reasons. For the word *symbol* is Greek, and it can be called also a norm and a bringing together; that is, they bring together what was many into one. The apostles composed it in these words by conferring as one and each one saying what he thought. It is therefore called a norm or a sign because at that time, as the apostle Paul says [see 2 Cor 11:13] and as it is referred to in the Acts of the Apostles [15:24], many were representing that they were apostles of Christ, calling Christ by name but not announcing the tradition in complete lines. For this reason, therefore, they put down this norm through which it is known

that the person was preaching Christ truly according to the apostolic standards. (4) And finally they note that this practice is observed also in civil wars, because [in these situations] the appearance of the arms is the same, and the sound of the voice is the same, and the way of living is one, and the   practices of fighting are the same. And, so that nothing might happen by a hidden trick, each leader gives different symbols to his soldiers, which in Latin are called either signs or proofs, so that if it should perchance occur that it was unclear who was who, the interrogated one might reveal the symbol to show if he was enemy or ally. For this reason finally [our fathers in the faith] handed over the Symbol, not written on pieces of parchment but as retained in the hearts, so that it would be certain that no one would know this by reading it, which situation sometimes also was in the habit of occurring with the unbelievers, but [in this way it would be known] that it had been disseminated from the tradition of the apostles.

(5) Therefore, as it has been said, as they were about to depart in order to preach, the apostles unanimously put together this norm of their faith.

The Symbol, therefore, is a sign through which God might be known, and thus the believing ones receive it so that they might know how they ought to prepare for contests of faith against the devil.

In the Symbol certainly there are few words, but all the mysteries are contained in it. For these things have been collected in brief form from all the Scriptures by the apostles so that, since many of the believers do not know how to read, or because those who do know how are not able to read the Scriptures because of the involvements of the world, by retaining these things in their heart they may have sufficient salutary knowledge for themselves. For the word of faith is brief and was once predicted by the prophet: "for the Lord will execute his sentence on the earth quickly and decisively" [Rom 9:28 (Vulgate)].[33]

XXIV (XXIII). THE RULE OF FAITH

(1) After the apostolic symbol, this is the most certain faith that our teachers have handed down:

We profess that the Father and the Son and the Holy Spirit are of one essence and of the same power and eternity, one God indivisible; so that, what is proper to each of the persons being preserved, the Trinity is not by any means to be divided in substance or in person. The Father is to be confessed as unbegotten, the Son as begotten. The Holy Spirit, however, is not begotten or unbegotten but proceeds from the Father and the Son. The Son proceeds, being born from the Father. The Holy Spirit proceeds, not having been born.

That the Son while perfect received humanity from the virgin without sin, so that he might mercifully repair the one he had created out of goodness alone, who had fallen freely. That he who was truly crucified rose on the third day and, glorified with the same flesh, ascended into heaven; in this flesh he is expected to come again to judge the living and the dead. (2) And that he carried a divine and human substance, perfect in both, one person, Christ, because he was not doubled in person by the integrity of the two substances nor mingled in a twofold substance by the unity of person. Neither is excluded by the other, because the one [person] preserved both [substances] by undefiled right.

That the salutary authority of the New and Old Testament is commended, the one truthfully fulfilled through prophecy, the other through history, and that neither about God nor about the creature of the world is it to be held with the pagans or with the heretics that there is anything among these things that dissents from the truth. (3) But that the divine utterances in both Testaments proclaim that this only is to be held: that out of no necessity did God create either man or the universe, or that there is any substance visible and invisible unless either it is God or it is the good created by the good God. (God is the supreme and unchangeable good; the creature truly is a lower and changeable good.) That the origin of souls is uncertain, and that the nature of angels or the soul is not part of the divine substance, but the creature was created by God out of nothing and therefore incorporeal because it was created in the image of God.

(4) Concerning the godliness of our ways of life,[34] without which the faith of the divine cult grows numb and with which the integrity of the divine cult is perfected—[this is our faith] that each one of us loving God for the sake of God and our neighbor in God, striving even to love also our enemies, may make progress so that by improving we might succeed.

That it is not possible for one to corrupt another by sin where consent is not given freely.

That legitimate marriages are not believed to be damned, although it is believed also that posterity born of them is subject to original sin, and it is taught in the law that the integrity of faithful and continent virgins is to be preferred to them.

(5) Neither is the one baptism of the Trinity repeated, because it is forbidden. Nor is it to be thought because of the diversity of ministers handing it down that it is being conferred by them, but that it is given by the power of God alone. About this we read what was said: "'He on whom you see the Spirit descend and remain is the one who baptizes with the Holy Spirit.' And I myself have seen and have testified that this is the Son of God'" [John 1:33–34].

And neither let us think that we do not need the remedies of penance for the daily excesses of human fragility, without which we are not able to exist in this life. Thus we ought to acknowledge that all sins are wiped away by the fruitful compunction of penance, as it is written: "Happy are those whose transgression is forgiven, whose sin is covered. Happy are those to whom the LORD imputes no iniquity" [Ps 31(32):1–2].

(6) It is also our faith that no one is placed under the headship of Christ by his own powers but through divine grace, and that by his persevering in unbroken peace in the unity of the church he is strengthened. Nor is anyone thought to be counted good by the power of human will, but all the number of the elect are acquired according to the purpose of God's will.

It is our faith that temporal goods are created by God both for the good and the bad, and his dispensation to each of these is either accepted or rejected. It is not the possession of these goods in anyone of the faithful, but their use that is to be judged either acceptable or unacceptable. It is our faith that only good people are able to reach the certain and eternal goods in the future. We believe that the church as now shaped is kept occupied as a guarantee of these goods, now having the firstfruits of the Spirit, in the future the perfection, now being sustained in hope, afterwards being fed on the reality, that now "we see indistinctly, as in a mirror"; in the future, however, "we shall see face to face" [1 Cor 13:12] when it shall be brought to light through faith. (7) It is our faith that until it is perfected in us so that we may enjoy the eternal goods of the most high God, we shall have learned that it is to be enjoyed in God and in our neighbors.

We have that hope in the resurrection by which we believe that we also shall be raised in the same order and in the same form in which the Lord himself rose from the dead, in the same body in which we are or have lived, not changing our nature or sex but only laying down our fragility and vices.

That Satan himself, with his angels and supporters, is to be condemned to eternal fire; and that according to their sacrilegious dispute, he is not to be restored to the original, that is, angelic, dignity from which he fell because of his own malice.

This is the true integrity of the tradition of the Catholic faith concerning which, if any one thing should be rejected, the whole credibility of the faith is lost.

XXV (XXIV). BAPTISM

(1) If I make known the sacrament of baptism, "tracing back to the very beginning,"[35] Moses baptized in the sea and in the cloud, both in a prefiguring and in symbol; for thus Paul pronounces [see 1 Cor 10:1–2]. Therefore the sea had the form of water; the cloud, that of the Holy Spirit; the manna, that of the bread of life. For in that sea, as the images of the fathers teach, the Egyptian is submerged, the people of God rise up, made new by the Holy Spirit, who also crossed through the Red Sea by an unobstructed step. John also baptized, but not wholly in a Jewish sense. For he baptized not only in water but also in spirit, but he only imparted this insofar as he baptized unto repentance, as Paul says in the Acts of the Apostles: "John baptized with the baptism of repentance" [Acts 19:4]. Nevertheless, therefore, it was given to him to baptize in water, so that Christ, who was about to baptize in water and in spirit, "might be revealed to Israel" [John 1:31] by the baptism of John. This occurred when he was plainly shown to all to be Son of God by the descent of the Holy Spirit and the voice of the Father. (2) Perfect baptism, therefore, began from Jesus. He baptized in the Holy Spirit before all else, even as John said: "I baptize with water. Among you stands one whom you do not know. He will baptize you with the Holy Spirit and fire" [John 1:26; Matt 3:11]. This is the perfection of baptism. It is God who baptizes so that those who are baptized are able to become sons of God.

There are three kinds of baptism: first, the baptism by which the stains of sin are washed away through the washing of regeneration. Second, the baptism by which one is baptized in his blood through martyrdom. By this baptism also Christ was baptized so that both in this, as in the others, he might give an example to the believers, as he was saying to his disciples the sons of Zebedee: "Are you able to drink the cup that I drink, or be baptized with the baptism that I am baptized with?" [Mark 10:38]. Therefore water and blood symbolize a twofold baptism: the one by which we are regenerated by a washing, the other by which we are consecrated by blood. (3) There is also a third baptism, of tears, which is accomplished laboriously, as the one who "every night...flood[s his] bed with tears" [Ps 6:7], who imitates the conversion of Manasseh and the humility of the people of Nineveh through which mercy followed, who imitates the prayer of that publican in the Temple, "who, standing far off, would not even look up to heaven, but was beating his breast" [Luke 18:13].

For the water of baptism is that which flowed from the side of Christ at the time of the passion, and there is no other element that purges all things in this world, that enlivens all things. Therefore, when we are baptized in Christ we are reborn through that water so that, purified, we might be brought to life.

(4) The font, however, is the origin of all glories. There are seven steps in it, three going down because of the three times in which we renounce, three others going up because of the three things which we confess. The seventh truly is he who is the fourth step, who "looks like the son of man" [Dan 3:32],[36] extinguishing the furnace of fire. He is the support of the steps, the foundation of the water, "For in [Christ] the whole fullness of deity dwells bodily" [Col 2:9].

The salutary gifts of baptism consist in the Father and the Son and the Holy Spirit. Thus, by no means is anyone sanctified by the ceremony of baptism unless one is washed under the sign of the Trinity, as the Lord says: "Go therefore and make disciples of all the nations, baptizing them in the name of the Father and of the Son and of the Holy Spirit" [Matt 28:19]. Consequently, if baptism should be given, a person of the Trinity having been omitted in any way, clearly nothing is done in the solemnity of regeneration unless the whole Trinity is invoked. (5) For even the Lord, when he was baptized by John, is read to have gone through this baptism under the sign of the Trinity. For with God saying: "This is my Son" [Matt 3:17], the Father was in the voice, the Son in the body; the Holy Spirit, however, is shown to have been in the form of the dove.

There are two covenants of the believers. The first covenant is that in which the devil and his pomps and his entire way of life are renounced. The second covenant is that in which it is professed that one believes in the Father and the Son and the Holy Spirit.

(6) It behooves us to be washed in Christ only once, because Christ also died only once for us. For if there is "one Lord" and "one faith," necessarily there is "one baptism" [Eph 4:5], because also there is one death of Christ for us. We are plunged into his image through the mystery of the sacred font, so that we might be buried with Christ, dying to this world, and from these same waters we emerge in the form of his resurrection, not to be returned to corruption, just as he was not returned to death. Because even if afterwards someone shall have been overtaken by some sin, he is expiated now not by the benefit of the washing but by repentance, which in imitation of the font puts sins to death.

(7) We believe that at the age of perfection baptism effects either the purgation of the original fault or the abolition of actual sin. For children, however, the effect of baptism is that they are washed only from the original sin that they contracted from Adam through their first birth. If they should have died before they are regenerated, without doubt they are separated from the kingdom of Christ, our savior testifying: "no one can enter the kingdom of God without being born of water and Spirit" [John 3:5]. Accordingly, children are baptized with another person professing, because as yet they do not know how to speak or believe. This is also the case with the sick, the speechless, and the deaf, on whose behalf another professes so as to respond on their behalf while they are being baptized. (8) However, although original sin passes away through the regeneration, nevertheless the punishment of the mandated death, which entered through the transgression, remains even in those whom the baptism of the savior cleanses from the fault of the origin. This is the case accordingly so that one will know that the hope of future happiness follows through regeneration, not so that he can be absolved from the punishment of temporal death.

As to the fact that it is not lawful for either private persons or clerics to baptize, but only priests, we read in the Gospel that it was permitted only for the apostles. For after the resurrection, Jesus said to them: "'As the Father has sent me, so I send you.' When he had said this, he breathed on them and said to them, 'Receive the Holy Spirit. If you forgive the sins of any, they are forgiven them; if you retain the sins of any, they are retained'" [John 20:21–23]. And in another place: "Go, therefore, and make disciples of all the nations, baptizing them in the name of the Father and of the Son and of the Holy Spirit" [Matt 28:19]. (9) Consequently, it remains unchanged that baptism is handed down by priests only. It is not licit for deacons to fulfill this ministry themselves apart from the bishop or a presbyter, unless, these being absent far away, the extreme necessity of sickness demands. Baptizing is also often permitted to the lay faithful, lest anyone be called from the world without this salutary remedy.

Heretics also, if nevertheless they were taught to have received baptism in attestation of the Father and the Son and the Holy Spirit, are not to be baptized again but are to be cleansed only by chrism and the imposition of hands. Baptism is not of man but of Christ, and therefore it is of no concern whether a heretic or a faithful one baptizes. (10) The sacrament is so sacred that it is not defiled by a murderer ministering it. Certainly a heretic has the baptism of Christ but, because he is outside the unity of the faith, it produces nothing for him. But when he shall have come back in, immediately the baptism that he had outside toward destruction begins now to work in him toward salvation. For the fact that he received it, I approve; that he received it outside the unity of faith, I disapprove. When he comes back in, however, he is not changed; he is recognized. Since the character [given him by baptism] is of my king, I will not be sacrilegious. I correct the deserter; I do not change the character.

XXVI (XXV). Chrism

(1) Moses joined and blended together the anointing with chrism first in Exodus, at the command of the Lord. Aaron and his sons were the first to be anointed with it in testimony of their priesthood and holiness. Afterwards also even kings were made sacred by this chrism. Thus, they were called "anointed ones,"[37] as it is written: "Do not touch my anointed ones" [Ps 104(105):15]. At that time there was only the mystical anointing of kings and priests by which Christ

was symbolized. Consequently also his name [Christ] is taken from the anointing with chrism.

(2) But now, after our Lord, true king and eternal priest, was anointed by God the Father with a heavenly and mystical anointing, not only bishops and kings but the entire church is consecrated by the anointing with chrism, because of the fact that the church is a limb of the eternal king and priest. Therefore, because we are a priestly and royal people [see 1 Pet 2:9], after the washing of baptism we are anointed so that we might be called by the name of Christ.

XXVII (XXVI). The Imposition of Hands or Confirmation

(1) Because after baptism the Holy Spirit is given through the bishops with the imposition of hands, we remember that the apostles had done this in the Acts of the Apostles. For this is what it says: "While Apollos was in Corinth, Paul passed through the interior regions and came to Ephesus, where he found some disciples. He said to them, 'Did you receive the Holy Spirit when you became believers?' They replied, 'No, we have not even heard that there is a Holy Spirit.' Then he said, 'Into what then were you baptized?' They answered, 'Into John's baptism.' Paul said, 'John baptized with the baptism of repentance, telling the people to believe in the one who was to come after him, that is, in Jesus.' On hearing this, they were baptized in the name of the Lord Jesus. When Paul had laid his hands on them, the Holy Spirit came upon them, and they spoke in tongues and prophesied" [Acts 19:1–6]. (2) Again in another place: "Now when the apostles at Jerusalem heard that Samaria had accepted the word of God, they sent Peter and John to them. The two went down and prayed for them that they might receive the Holy Spirit (for as yet the Spirit had not come upon any of them; they had only been baptized in the name of the Lord Jesus). Then Peter and John laid their hands on them, and they received the Holy Spirit" [Acts 8:14–17]. (3) Consequently, we are able to receive the Holy Spirit, we are not able to give him, but we ask the Lord that he be given.

Let me add, however, by whom this is done most especially, as holy Pope Innocent wrote.[38] He stated that it is permitted to be done by a bishop and not by any other. For presbyters, although they are priests, nevertheless do not have the summit of the episcopacy. (4) It is obligatory that only bishops do the sealing and hand on the Holy Spirit. Not only does ecclesiastical custom demonstrate this, but so also the above-cited reading from the Acts of the Apostles, which asserts that Peter and John were those who were directed to hand on the Holy Spirit to the already baptized. Although it is permitted to priests either without a bishop, or with a bishop present, to anoint the baptized with chrism when they baptize, they may do so only with chrism that has been consecrated by the bishop. Nevertheless, they are not to sign the forehead with that oil, because that ought to be done only by bishops when they hand on the Holy Spirit.

(5) These are a few of the many teachings of more credible men that we have come to understand. Consequently, it will be seen that we have interjected their comments in certain places, so that our discourse might be strengthened by statements of the fathers.

THE END

NOTES

INTRODUCTION

1. Christopher M. Lawson, ed., *St. Isidore, Bishop of Seville's De Ecclesiasticis Officiis,* Corpus Christianorum, Series Latina 113 (Brepols: Turnholt, 1989) (hereafter DEO).

2. Ibid., "Preface," 7*–11*.

3. Ibid. See "Liminaire," 5*.

4. This introduction is written in collaboration with Raúl Gómez-Ruiz, SDS, PhD. Unless otherwise noted, translations in this introduction from Spanish or Latin to English are by Gómez. Some of the material on the Hispano-Mozarabic Eucharist can also be found in Raúl Gómez-Ruiz, *Mozarabs, Hispanics, and the Cross,* Studies in Latino/a Catholicism (Maryknoll, NY: Orbis Books, 2007).

5. Jacques Fontaine, *Isidore de Seville: Genèse et originalité de la culture hispanique au temps des Wisigoths* (Brepols: Turnhout, 2000); Fray Justo Pérez de Urbel, *San Isidoro de Sevilla: Su Vida, Su Obra Y Su Tiempo,* 3rd ed. (León: Universidad de León, 1995); U. D. del Val, "Isidoro de Sevilla," *Diccionario de Historia Eclesiástica de España,* dirigido por Quintín Aldea Vaquero, Tomás Marín Martínez, José Vives Gatell, 4 vols. (Madrid: Instituto Enrique Flórez, 1972), vol. 2; Antonio Vinayo González, *San Isidoro de Sevilla: Su Doctrina y Su Pensamiento en 500 Aforismos y Sentencias* (León: Editorial Isidoriana, 2000).

6. Pérez de Urbel (*San Isidoro,* 23) maintains that Isidore was born in 556, two years after the Byzantines took possession of Cartagena.

7. Fontaine, *Isidore de Seville,* 89; cf. Pérez de Urbel, *San Isidoro,* 27, who claims that Turtur was the family's nursemaid.

8. Pérez de Urbel, *San Isidoro,* 22.

9. Roger Collins, *Early Medieval Spain: Unity in Diversity, 400–1000* (New York: St. Martin's Press, 1983), 61.

10. Jaime Vicens Vives, *Approaches to the History of Spain,* 2nd ed., corrected and revised, trans. and ed. Joan Connelly Ullman (Berkeley: University of California Press, 1970; 1st ed. 1967; originally published as *Aproximación a la historia de España* [Barcelona: Editorial Vicens-Vives, 1952]; English trans.

based on the 2nd ed., published by Editorial Teide, 1960, for the Centro de Estudios Históricos Internacionales, Universidad de Barcelona), 25.

11. Lawson, *St. Isidore*, 15*. Lawson's critical edition demonstrates that DEO 1, 3–18 is arranged in an order suggested by the pattern of the Spanish liturgy.

12. Pérez de Urbel, *San Isidoro*, 275–77.

13. See Fontaine, *Isidore de Seville*, 406; M. C. Díaz y Díaz, *Index Scriptorum Latinorum Medii Aevi Hispanorum* (Salamanca: Universidad de Salamanca, 1959), 30; Gordon B. Ford, Jr., ed. *The Letters of St. Isidore of Seville*, 2nd rev. ed. (Amsterdam: A. M. Hakkert, 1970), 7.

14. See listing in Fontaine, *Isidore de Seville*, 436–37.

15. Ibid., 284–85.

16. *Iberian Fathers*, vol. 2, trans. Claude Barlow, Fathers of the Church 63 (Washington, DC: Catholic University of America Press, 1969), 140. The Latin text and French translation appear in Fontaine, *Isidore de Seville*, 431–35.

17. DEO, 19*–134*. Lawson's exhaustive study of the manuscripts for just this one work demonstrates clearly the widespread provenance of Isidore's works throughout Europe.

18. Fontaine, *Isidore de Seville*, 217, 436.

19. See Lawson, *St. Isidore*, 13*–14*, for the evidence for dating DEO between 598 and 618.

20. See Barlow's translation of the *Renotatio* by Braulio, *Iberian Fathers*, 2:140–42.

21. Edward P. Colbert, *Martyrs of Cordoba (850–859): A Study of the Sources*, Studies in Medieval History n.s. 17 (Washington, DC: Catholic University of America Press, 1962), 33.

22. Jocelyn N. Hillgarth, *Visigothic Spain, Byzantium, and the Irish* (London: Variorum Reprints, 1985), vii.

23. Ibid., vii–viii.

24. Yves M.-J. Congar, *Revue du Moyen Age latin (RMAL)* [Lyon-Strasbourg] 8 (1952): 27ff., cited in Jocelyn N. Hillgarth, "The Position of Isidorian Studies: A Critical Review of the Literature, 1936–1975," *Studi Medievali*, Ser 3, 24 (1983): 883: "a master of logical discourse and of definitions, one of the first teachers to teach the reasoned use of his language…an instrument of order, and within limits, of precision of thought" (trans. by Knoebel).

25. Ibid.

26. Rachel L. Stocking, *Bishops, Councils, and Consensus in the Visigothic Kingdom, 589–633* (Ann Arbor: University of Michigan Press, 2000), 21.

27. Ibid., 13. Stocking notes in n. 49 that the fundamental modern work on Isidore and his cultural project is Jacques Fontaine, *Isidore de Seville et la culture classique dans l'Espagne wisigothique*, 2 vols. (Paris: Etudes Augustiniennes, 1959).

28. Stocking, *Bishops, Councils*, 13.

29. See "El Concilio III de Toledo: Texto Crítico," *Concilio III de Toledo: XIV Centenario 589–1989* (Toledo: Arzobispado de Toledo, 1991), 13–38.

30. Stocking, *Bishops, Councils,* 27.

31. Ibid., 28–29.

32. Ibid., 29.

33. Raúl R. Gómez, SDS, "Lignum Crucis: The Cross in the Good Friday Celebration of the Hispano-Mozarabic Triduum" (PhD diss., Catholic University of America, Washington, DC, 2001), 67.

34. Antonio Viñayo González, preface to Pérez de Urbel, *San Isidoro,* 6.

35. Hillgarth, "Position of Isidorian Studies," 837.

36. See Fontaine, *Isidore de Seville,* 199.

37. Lawson, *St. Isidore,* 14*–15*, 119*–21*.

38. Ibid., 15*.

39. Ibid.

40. See Fontaine, *Isidore de Seville,* 201.

41. Hillgarth, "Position of Isidorian Studies," 850.

42. The major sources used by Isidore are listed at the conclusion of this introduction.

43. See Hillgarth, *Visigothic Spain, Byzantium, and the Irish.*

44. Fontaine, *Isidore de Seville,* 203. The extant *acta* are in José Vives, Tomás Marín Martínez, and Gonzalo Martínez Díez, eds., *Concilios Visigóticos e Hispano-Romanos,* España Cristiana 1 (Barcelona/Madrid: Consejo Superior de Investigaciones Científicas Instituto Enrique Flórez, 1963), canon 13, 196.

45. See Michael Witczak, "The Sacramentary of Paul VI," in *The Eucharist,* vol. 3, *Handbook for Liturgical Studies,* ed. Anscar J. Chupungco (Collegeville, MN: A Pueblo Book, Liturgical Press, 1999), 146.

46. Fontaine, *Isidore de Seville,* 204.

47. Ibid., 207.

48. Simon J. Keay, *Roman Spain,* Exploring the Roman World 2 (Berkeley: University of California Press/British Museum, 1988), 8.

49. Joseph F. O'Callaghan, *A History of Medieval Spain* (Ithaca, NY/London: Cornell University Press, 1975; repr., Cornell Paperbacks, 1994), 28.

50. Ibid., 32; Teodoro González, "Paganismo, judaísmo, herejías y relaciones con el exterior," in *Historia de la Iglesia en España,* vol. 1, *La Iglesia en la España romana y visigoda,* Biblioteca de Autores Cristianos 16 (Madrid: Edica, 1979), 697–98.

51. Henri Leclercq and Fernand Cabrol, "Mozarabe (La Liturgie)," *Dictionnaire d'Archéologie Chrétienne et de Liturgie,* ed. Fernand Cabrol and Henri Leclercq (Paris: Librairie Letouzey et Ané, 1935), vol. 2-A, p. 391.

52. Conferencia Episcopal Española, "Prenotandos," no. 2, *Missale Hispano-Mozarabicum,* vol. 1 (Toledo: Arzobispado de Toledo, 1991), 15–58.

53. Mary Collins, OSB, "Language, Liturgical," in *New Dictionary of*

Sacramental Worship (Collegeville, MN: Liturgical Press, A Michael Glazier Book, 1990), 653.

54. Josef A. Jungmann, SJ, *The Early Liturgy to the Time of Gregory the Great*, trans. Francis A. Brunner, CSsR, University of Notre Dame Liturgical Studies 6 (1959; repr., Notre Dame, IN: University of Notre Dame Press, 1980), 227.

55. See T. González, "Paganismo," 689–97.

56. See Jaime Colomina Torner, "1992: Toledo Mozárabe en Roma," *Toletum* 28 (1992): 154–55.

57. Ibid., 157. Nonetheless, a posthumous publication on the rite by the foremost expert on the rite, Dom Jordi Pinell I Pons, OSB, uses the term *liturgia hispánica* (Hispanic liturgy) almost exclusively. See Jordi Pinell, *Liturgia hispánica*, ed. José Aldazábal, Biblioteca litúrgica 9 (Barcelona: Centre de Pastoral Litúrgica, 1998).

58. Cited in *Crónica Mozárabe* no. 8 (1982): 2: "sin olvidar que en la liturgia postconciliar el canto del Padrenuestro en toda España es precisamente el de la liturgia mozárabe."

59. See "The Lord's Prayer," alternate version, Appendix 3, *Roman Missal*, Revised by decree of the Second Vatican Council and Published by Authority of Pope Paul VI: *The Sacramentary*, approved for use in the Dioceses of the United States of America by the National Conference of Catholic Bishops and Confirmed by the Apostolic See, Eng. trans. prep. by ICEL (New York: Catholic Book Pub. Co., 1985), 1043.

60. "Homilía de S.S. Juan Pablo II en la Basílica de San Pedro durante la Misa en Rito Hispano-Mozárabe," *Boletín Oficial del Arzobispado de Toledo* 148 (1992): 275–79: "La liturgia hispano-mozárabe representa pues una realidad eclesial, y también cultural, que no puede ser relegada al olvido si se quiere comprender en profundidad las raíces del espíritu cristiano del pueblo español."

61. Ramón Gonzálvez Ruiz (Gonzálvez), "Cisneros y la Reforma del Rito Hispano-Mozárabe" (paper presented at the International Colloquium on the Bible and the Spanish Renaissance: Cardinal Ximénez de Cisneros (1436–1517) and the Complutensian Polyglot, Loyola University Chicago, Water Tower Campus, June 10–13, 1999; text provided by Gonzálvez), 33–38.

62. J. M. Pinell, "Los textos de la antigua liturgia hispánica: Fuentes para su estudio," *Estudios sobre la liturgia mozárabe* [Toledo] (1965): 109–64.

63. Pinell, *Liturgia hispánica*, 28–29; Josef A. Jungmann, SJ, *The Place of Christ in Liturgical Prayer*, trans. Geoffrey Chapman (Collegeville, MN: Liturgical Press, 1989), 221.

64. Leclercq and Cabrol, "Mozarabe (La Liturgie)," 483: "On y trouve de véritables thèses de théologie avec tous leurs développements."

65. "Prenotandos," no. 8; Pinell, *Liturgia hispánica*, 28–29; Manuel Sotomayor y Muro (Sotomayor), "La Iglesia hispana en la época de transi-

ción," in *Historia de la Iglesia en España*, vol. 1, *La Iglesia en la España romana y visigoda*, Biblioteca de Autores Cristianos 16 (Madrid: Edica, 1979), 386.

66. "Prenotandos," no. 2.

67. See Pinell, *Liturgia hispánica*, 28; Sotomayor, "La Iglesia hispana," 390–400; Teodoro González, "Vida cristiana y cura pastoral," in *Historia* (as in n. 65), 579–85.

68. "Prenotandos," no. 8: "Esto explicará que en las fuentes que han llegado hasta nosotros deba reconocerse la existencia de dos tradiciones distintas."

69. Ibid., nos. 15 and 16. Pinell, *Liturgia hispánica*, 39–40. He was also the primary author of the "Prenotandos"; see José Aldazábal, "Presentación," in *Liturgia hispánica*, ed. José Aldazábal, Biblioteca litúrgica 9 (Barcelona: Centre de Pastoral Litúrgica, 1998), 12; also J. M. Pinell, "Missale Hispano-Mozarabicum," *Notitiæ* 24 (1988): 670–727.

70. "Prenotandos," nos. 9 and 15.

71. "Prenotandos," no. 16.

72. See Keay, *Roman Spain*, 62–63, 179.

73. Pinell, *Liturgia hispánica*, 39–40; also idem, "El problema de las dos tradiciones del antiguo rito hispánico: Valoración documental de la tradición B, en vistas a una eventual revisión del Ordinario de la Misa Mozárabe," in *Liturgia y Música Mozárabes: Ponencias y Comunicaciones presentadas al I Congreso Internacional de Estudios Mozárabes: Toledo, 1975*, Serie D, 1 (Toledo: Instituto de Estudios Visigóticos-Mozárabes de San Eugenio, 1978), 26–27. Cf. José Janini, "Libros Litúrgicos mozárabes de Toledo conquistado," in *Estudios Sobre Alfonso VI y la Reconquista de Toledo: Actas del II Congreso Internacional de Estudios Mozárabes (Toledo, 20–26 Mayo 1985)* Serie Histórica 5 (Toledo: Instituto de Estudios Visigótico-Mozárabes, 1990), 4:10–11.

74. See, e.g., Pinell, "El problema de las dos tradiciones," 26, 28; Janini, "Libros Litúrgicos mozárabes," 17–18: Janini cites Archbishop Rodrigo Ximénez de Rada's *De Rebus Hispaniæ* (1243) and Pedro López de Ayala's *Crónica del rey don Pedro* (c. 1400) as indicators of this attribution.

75. Janini, "Libros Litúrgicos mozárabes," 17–18. On p. 17 n. 25 he cites *De Rebus Hispaniæ*, lib. III, cap. 3: ed. Lorenzana, *Patres Toletanorum* 3 (Madrid, 1793), 77, which declares that six parishes in Toledo were still celebrating rites in the thirteenth century, attributed to Isidore and Leander: permisi sunt uti lege et ecclesiasticis institutis et habere pontifices et evangelicos sacerdotes, apud quos viguit officium Isidori et Leandri, et viget hodie in sex parroquiis toletanis ("In six parishes of Toledo, they are still permitted today, according to ecclesiastical laws and norms, to have both bishops and evangelical priests, who follow the offices of Isidore and Leander").

76. Pinell, *Liturgia hispánica*, 39.

77. Julio González, "Los mozárabes toledanos desde el siglo XI hasta el Cardenal Cisneros," in *Historia Mozárabe, Primer Congreso Internacional de*

Estudios Mozárabes: Toledo, 1975, Serie C, no. 1 (Toledo: Instituto de Estudios Visigótico-Mozárabes de San Eugenio, 1978), 82.

78. Cf. Pinell, *Liturgia hispánica*, 40; Janini, "Libros Litúrgicos mozárabes," 14–16. Janini attributes some of these manuscripts to the mid-thirteenth century.

79. Pinell, *Liturgia hispánica*, 39.

80. Ibid., 40.

81. An original edition of the *Missale mixtum secundum regulam beati Isidori dictum Mozarabes* (1500) rests in the library of the Museo del Hospital de la Santa Cruz, Toledo (Inventory no. 1324, possession of the parish of Santas Justa y Rufina).

82. Ramón Gonzálvez, "Noticias sobre códices mozárabes en los antiguos inventarios de la Biblioteca Capitular de Toledo," in *Historia Mozárabe* (see n. 77 above), 77.

83. Ibid., 75, 77. Gonzálvez notes that only twenty-nine Mozarabic manuscripts are still in the Capitular Archives and Library at Toledo.

84. See "Prenotandos," nos. 2 and 9.

85. Cyrille Vogel, *Medieval Liturgy: An Introduction to the Sources*, rev. and trans. William G. Storey and Niels Krogh Rasmussen, OP, with the assistance of John K. Brooks-Leonard (Washington, DC: Pastoral Press, 1986; rev. and updated from *Introduction aux sources de l'histoire du culte chrétien au moyen age*, 1981), 38.

86. "Prenotandos," no. 9; Vogel, *Medieval Liturgy*, 36; Marius Férotin, *Le Liber Mozarabicus Sacramentorum et les Manuscrits Mozarabes*, Monumenta Ecclesiae Liturgica 6 (Paris: Firmin-Didot, 1912), xvii; Juan Francisco Rivera Recio, "La Iglesia mozárabe," in *Historia de la Iglesia en España*, vol. 2, pt. 1, *La Iglesia de los siglos VIII al XIV*, Biblioteca de Autores Cristianos 17 (Madrid: Edica, 1982), 29.

87. Férotin, *Liber Mozarabicus*, xix.

88. P. M. Gy, "History of the Liturgy in the West to the Council of Trent," in *Principles of the Liturgy*, vol. 1, *The Church at Prayer: An Introduction to the Liturgy* (one vol. ed.), ed. A. G. Martimort, trans. Matthew J. O'Connell with an introduction by Gerald S. Sloyan (Collegeville, MN: Liturgical Press, 1992), 54.

89. See also Jungmann's discussion of certain Hispano-Mozarabic prayers and their incorporation into the Roman liturgy (*Early Liturgy*, 230).

90. Thomas E. Burman, *Religious Polemic and the Intellectual History of the Mozarabs, c. 1050–1200*, Brill's Studies in Intellectual History 52 (Leiden: E. J. Brill, 1994), 18, 19–22.

91. See, e.g., Rose Walker, *Views of Transition: Liturgy and Illumination in Medieval Spain*, British Library Studies in Medieval Culture (Toronto/Buffalo: University of Toronto Press, 1998), 23.

92. See Marius Férotin, "Introduction," in *Le Liber Ordinum en Usage dans l'Église Wisigothique et Mozarabe d'Espagne du Cinquième Siècle*, Monumenta

Ecclesiae Liturgica 5 (Paris: Firmin-Didot, 1904), xi–xxxvii; and idem, "Introduction," in *Liber Mozarabicus*, xliii. Also see José Janini, "Introducción," xvii–lxxvii, *Liber Missarum de Toledo*, vol. 2, Serie Litúrgica, fuentes IV–VIII (Toledo: Instituto de Estudios Visigótico-Mozárabes, 1983), 303.

93. Pinell, *Liturgia Hispánica*, 39.

94. A. C. Lawson, "The Sources of the *De Ecclesiasticis Officiis* of St. Isidore of Seville" (Oxford thesis for the D.D. [Bodl. MS, Eng. Theol. C. 56], 1937).

95. Hillgarth, "Position of Isidorian Studies," 850.

96. Lawson, *St. Isidore*, "Index Scriptorum," 151–57.

BOOK I: *DE ECCLESIASTICIS OFFICIIS*

1. There is a discrepancy in the critical text. Several manuscripts divide this chapter into two, inserting a chapter titled "On the Sabbath." Lawson opts to follow this manuscript tradition in the text, but not in the listing of the chapters. As a result, the text is actually divided into forty-five chapters. Thus in the above listing, chapter twenty-five is actually chapter twenty-six in the text. This change affects the numbering of each subsequent chapter.

2. *Ecclesia*, assembly.

3. Isidore's Latin is *oratorum*, lit., "those who pray."

4. Augustine *Confessions* 10.50.

5. See C. M. Lawson, ed., Sancti Isidori Episcopi Hispalensis, *De Ecclesiasticis Officiis*, Corpus Christianorum, Series Latina 113 (Turnholt: Brepols, 1989), 9, 110. Subsequent references to this work are given as "Lawson" plus page number.

6. Lawson (p. 11) and various manuscripts are aware of this error.

7. Here Isidore introduces [up to end of section (2)] material derived from tractate *Baba Bathra* in the *Babylonian Talmud;* see A. C. Lawson, in *Revue Bénédictine*, 50 (1938): 26.

8. Augustine *De doctrina christiana* 2.11.16.

9. The Vulgate has "on your holy mountain" instead of "to your holy name."

10. The reference is to Cassian.

11. Latin: *Laus dei.*

12. *Doctores*, that is, the experts, authorities, doctors of the faith.

13. *Hispaniarum*, literally, peoples of Hispania.

14. Lawson uses *inlatio*. In the Hispano-Mozarabic Eucharist, the name of this prayer is *illatio*. It functions as an equivalent of the Roman rite Preface prayer.

15. Cyprian *Letter to Cecil, Epistula* 63.2, 13.

16. Augustine *Enchiridion* 29.110.

17. Vulgate; my translation.

18. See Lawson's note regarding the proper form of this word (p. 114).

19. Cassian *De institutis coenobiorum* 3.3.10; 3.4.1 *(Corpus scriptorum ecclesiasticorum latinorum* 17:38).

20. See Lawson, 28, where he states in Latin, "before this word *(sabbatum)* [various manuscripts] place the title *De sabbato.* They thus divide one chapter into two parts. We have not corrected this error, lest the studious be deceived." Also see n. 1 above.

21. Vulgate; my translation.

22. Cassian *Conferences* 10.2.1–2.

23. The Nicene Creed.

24. Latin: *passio.*

25. Latin: *transitus.*

26. The ancients considered March the first month of the year.

27. 7 x 7 = 49(50).

28. "Sevens" in the text.

29. Gregory Nazianzen.

30. Cassian *Conferences* 21.20.3.

31. The actual Greek word may be *kainos.* It is not clear whether Isidore has transliterated the Greek into Latin or if *cenon* is an error. Lawson does not comment on this point.

32. In Latin, *quadragenarius* is the word for "forty" and *denarius* the word for "money." It appears that Isidore has made a word association here.

33. Cassian *Conferences* 21.29.1.

34. See Lawson, 118, for his preference for "seventh month" as the proper translation. Nevertheless, starting with March as the first month, September is the seventh.

35. See Lawson, 118: "handed down the memory of him."

BOOK II: *DE ECCLESIASTICIS OFFICIIS*

1. Lawson indicates that in the two editions of Grial and Arévalo, a chapter XIV "Acolytes" (originally from *Etymologies* VII,12,29–30) has been inserted. Since most references to DEO follow these editions, he has resolved the issue by not including the chapter in the text, numbering the chapters here as they appeared in Isidore's work, but numbering the chapters in the text as they are in Grial and Arévalo, adding the correct enumeration in brackets following. See Lawson, 8*, and notes on 52 and 73.

2. The state of being named by lot.

3. One named by lot.

4. *Acephali*, that is, those without an ecclesiastical superior.

5. Virgil *Aeneid* 6.25.

6. Several manuscripts place the beginning of the chapter here. Lawson places it after the next sentence. See his note on p. 56.

7. See also Lev 8:2–13. Lawson cites Exod 28:4–9.

8. A priestly garment reaching to the ankle.

9. The phrase is often used in regard to sins confessed in the sacrament of penance. In the past, a letter, for example, could be sealed (by wax and the imprint of the ring) and could be opened only by the one to whom it was directed. In the case of sins confessed in the confessional, this one is God only, thus the phrase "the seal of the confessional."

10. The Latin is *magisterium sacerdotii.*

11. At this time, mortal sin was seen as a fairly restrictive term, for example, adultery, apostasy, and murder.

12. The word used for "bishop" is *episkopos.*

13. Lawson, 121 (II, 9, 4), discusses the correct title of this man. He agrees with the source (Numbers) and with the *Liber Ordinum* that he is a guardian of sacred things, not of the sacristy (as Isidore calls him). However, the rubric in the *Liber Ordinum* calls him the *sacrista* (the sacristan) so the idea is obviously much the same.

14. For use at the *Lavabo* at Mass.

15. For numbering of this and subsequent chapters, see note 1 above in listing of chapters.

16. Cassian *Conferences* 18.8.1–2.

17. Isidore calls them *circelliones.*

18. That is, relics.

19. This category of monks is mentioned in Jerome *Epistulai* 22.34; Cassian *Conferences* 18.4.7; and the Rule of St. Benedict (ch. 1). All describe it in negative terms.

20. Isidore calls them *renuitae.*

21. Jerome *Epistle* 22.34.

22. Cassian *Conferences* 18.9–10.

23. "The word *celuma* refers to that co-ordination of effort afforded by the leader's call to time the stroke for oarsmen." Mary Sarah Muldowney, trans., "The Work of Monks," *Saint Augustine: Treatises on Various Subjects,* Fathers of the Church 16 (New York: Fathers of the Church, 1952), 363 n. 1.

24. *Abba* or abbot.

25. The Latin is *mafortem* from *mafors,* viz., "Mavors" (ancient form for Mars).

26. The god of agriculture and war.

27. Theophrastus, according to Lawson.

28. Augustine, whom Isidore is citing here, is referring to the procedures of Roman civil law, as there was at that date no specifically Christian form or rite

of marriage. So Edmund Hill, OP, trans., *The Works of St Augustine: Sermons I (1–19) On the Old Testament* (Brooklyn, NY: New City Press, 1990), 281 n. 45.

29. See Jerome *Commentaries on Matthew* 3.19.9.

30. Lactantius *Divine Institutes* 6.23.23–25.

31. Isidore uses the word *lunaticus,* literally "lunatic."

32. Their sponsors.

33. See Isa 10:23 for source verse.

34. According to Lawson (p. 126), this section, "Concerning the Godliness of Our Ways of Life" extends through the end of the first sentence of (7).

35. Virgil *Aeneid* 1.372.

36. The Vulgate has "son of God."

37. In Latin the word for anointed is *christus.*

38. Innocent *Epistle* 25.3, 6 (*Patrologia cursus completus: Series latina,* ed. J.-P. Migne [Paris, 1844–64], 20:554–55).

SELECTED BIBLIOGRAPHY

Aldazábal, José. "Presentación." In *Liturgia hispánica*, edited by José Aldazábal, 9–12. Biblioteca litúrgica 9. Barcelona: Centre de Pastoral Litúrgica, 1998.

Barlow, Claude W., trans. *Iberian Fathers*, Volume 2, *Braulio of Saragossa, Fructuosus of Braga*. Fathers of the Church 63. Washington, DC: Catholic University of America Press, 1969.

Burman, Thomas E. *Religious Polemic and the Intellectual History of the Mozarabs, c. 1050–1200*. Brill's Studies in Intellectual History 52. Leiden: E. J. Brill, 1994.

Cazier, Pierre. *Isidore de Seville et la Naissance de L'Espagne Catholique*. Théologie Historique 96. Paris: Beauchesne, 1994.

Colbert, Edward P. *The Martyrs of Cordoba (850–859): A Study of the Sources*. Studies in Mediaeval History, n.s. 17. Washington, DC: Catholic University of America Press, 1962.

Collins, Mary, OSB. "Language, Liturgical." In *New Dictionary of Sacramental Worship*, 651–61. Collegeville, MN: Liturgical Press, A Michael Glazier Book, 1990.

Collins, Roger. *Early Medieval Spain: Unity in Diversity, 400–1000*. New York: St. Martin's Press, 1983.

Colomina Torner, Jaime (Colomina). "1992: Toledo Mozárabe en Roma." *Toletum* 28 (1992): 153–59.

"El Concilio III de Toledo. Texto Crítico," 13–38. *Concilio III de Toledo: XIV Centenario 589–1989*. Toledo: Arzobispado de Toledo, 1991.

Conferencia Episcopal Española. "Prenotandos." *Missale Hispano-Mozarabicum*, 1:15–58. Toledo: Arzobispado de Toledo, 1991.

Díaz y Díaz, Manuel C. *Index Scriptorum Latinorum Medii Aevi Hispanorum*. Madrid: University of Salamanca, 1959.

———. *Isidoriana: Estudios sobre San Isidoro de Sevilla en el XIV Centenario de su nacimiento*. León: Centro de Estudios "San Isidoro," 1961.

Diesner, Hans-Joachim. *Isidor von Sevilla und das Westgotische Spanien*. Trier: Spee-Verlag, 1978.

Férotin, Marius. *Le Liber Mozarabicus Sacramentorum et les Manuscrits Mozarabes*. Monumenta Ecclesiae Liturgica 6. Paris: Firmin-Didot, 1912.

———. *Le Liber Ordinum en Usage dans l'Église Wisigothique et Mozarabe d'Espagne du Cinquième Siècle*. Monumenta Ecclesiae Liturgica 5. Paris: Firmin-Didot, 1904.

Fontaine, Jacques. *Isidore de Seville et la culture classique dans l'Espagne Wisigothique*. 2nd ed. 2 vols. Paris: Etudes Augustiniennes, 1983.

————. *Isidore de Seville: Genèse et originalité de la culture hispanique au temps des Wisigoths*. Turnhout: Brepols, 2000.

Ford, Gordon B., Jr., ed. *The Letters of St. Isidore of Seville*. Translated from the Latin with an introduction. 2nd rev. ed. Amsterdam: Adolf M. Hakkert, 1970.

Gómez, Raúl R., SDS [Gómez-Ruiz]. "Lignum Crucis: The Cross in the Good Friday Celebration of the Hispano-Mozarabic Triduum." PhD diss., Catholic University of America, Washington, DC, 2001.

————. *Mozarabs, Hispanics, and the Cross*. Maryknoll, NY: Orbis Books, 2007.

González, Julio. "Los mozárabes toledanos desde el siglo XI hasta el Cardenal Cisneros." In *Historia Mozárabe, Primer Congreso Internacional de Estudios Mozárabes: Toledo, 1975*, 79–90. Serie C, no. 1. Toledo: Instituto de Estudios Visigótico-Mozárabes de San Eugenio, 1978.

González, Teodoro. "La Conversión de los Visigodos al Catolicismo." In *Historia de la Iglesia en España*, vol. 1, *La iglesia en la España romana y visigoda*, 402–21. Biblioteca de Autores Cristianos 16. Madrid: Edica, 1979.

————. "Organización de la Iglesia Visigoda." In *Historia de la Iglesia en España*, vol. 1, *La iglesia en la España romana y visigoda*, 491–535. Biblioteca de Autores Cristianos 16. Madrid: Edica, 1979.

————. "Paganismo, judaísmo, herejías y relaciones con el exterior." In *Historia de la Iglesia en España*, vol. 1, *La iglesia en la España romana y visigoda*, 663–99. Biblioteca de Autores Cristianos 16. Madrid: Edica, 1979.

————. "Vida cristiana y cura pastoral." In *Historia de la Iglesia en España*, vol. 1, *La iglesia en la España romana y visigoda*, 564–611. Biblioteca de Autores Cristianos 16. Madrid: Edica, 1979.

Gonzálvez Ruiz, Ramón (Gonzálvez). "Cisneros y la Reforma del Rito Hispano-Mozárabe." Paper presented at the International Colloquium on the Bible and the Spanish Renaissance: Cardinal Ximénez de Cisneros (1436–1517) and the Complutensian Polyglot, Loyola University Chicago, Water Tower Campus, June 10–13, 1999. Text provided by author.

————. "Noticias sobre códices mozárabes en los antiguos inventarios de la Biblioteca Capitular de Toledo." In *Historia Mozárabe, Primer Congreso Internacional de Estudios Mozárabes: Toledo, 1975*, 45–78. Serie C, no. 1. Toledo: Instituto de Estudios Visigótico-Mozárabes de San Eugenio, 1978.

Gy, P. M. "History of the Liturgy in the West to the Council of Trent." In *Principles of the Liturgy*, vol. 1, *The Church at Prayer: An Introduction to the Liturgy* (one vol. ed.), edited by A. G. Martimort, translated by Matthew

J. O'Connell with an introduction by Gerard S. Sloyan, 45–61. Collegeville, MN: Liturgical Press, 1992. This entirely new edition contains the 1983 translation of the four-volume paperback edition that appeared in French in the 1960s.

Henderson, John. *The Medieval World of Isidore of Seville: Truth from Words.* Cambridge: Cambridge University Press, 2007.

Hill, Edmund, OP, trans. and notes. *The Works of St Augustine: Sermons I (1–19) On the Old Testament.* Brooklyn, NY: New City Press, 1990.

Hillgarth, Jocelyn N. "Isidorian Studies (1976–1985)." *Studi Medievali,* Ser 3, 31, no. 2 (Spoleto, 1990): 925–73.

————. "Popular Religion in Visigothic Spain." In *Visigothic Spain: New Approaches,* edited by Edward James, 3–60. Oxford: Oxford University Press, 1980.

————. "The Position of Isidorian Studies: A Critical Review of the Literature, 1936–1975." *Studi Medievali,* Ser 3, 24 (1983): 818–905.

————. *Visigothic Spain, Byzantium, and the Irish.* London: Variorum Reprints, 1985.

"Homilía de S.S. Juan Pablo II en la Basílica de San Pedro durante la Misa en Rito Hispano-Mozárabe." *Boletín Oficial del Arzobispado de Toledo* 148 (1992): 275–79.

Janini, José. "Introducción." In *Liber Missarum de Toledo,* xvii–lxxvii. Vol. 2. Serie Litúrgica, fuentes IV–VIII. Toledo: Instituto de Estudios Visigótico-Mozárabes, 1983.

————. "Libros Litúrgicos mozárabes de Toledo conquistado." In *Estudios Sobre Alfonso VI y la Reconquista de Toledo: Actas del II Congreso Internacional de Estudios Mozárabes (Toledo, 20-26 Mayo 1985),* 4:9–25. Serie Histórica 5. Toledo: Instituto de Estudios Visigótico-Mozárabes, 1990.

————. "Introducción." In *Liber Misticus de Cuaresma y Pascua (Cod. Toledo, Bibl. Capit. 35.5),* xv–xxxvi. Serie Litúrgica, Fuentes II. Toledo: Instituto de Estudios Visigótico-Mozárabes, 1980.

Jungmann, Josef A., SJ. *The Early Liturgy to the Time of Gregory the Great.* Translated by Francis A. Brunner, CSsR. University of Notre Dame Liturgical Studies 6. 1959. Reprint, Notre Dame, IN: University of Notre Dame Press, 1980.

————. *The Place of Christ in Liturgical Prayer.* Translated by Geoffrey Chapman. Collegeville, MN: Liturgical Press, 1989.

Keay, S. J. *Roman Spain.* Exploring the Roman World 2. Berkeley: University of California Press/British Museum, 1988.

Lawson, Christopher M., ed. Sancti Isidori Episcopi Hispalensis, *De Ecclesiasticis Officiis.* Corpus Christianorum, Series Latina 113, Isidori Episcopi Hispalensis Opera. Turnholt: Brepols, 1989.

Leclercq, Henri, and Fernand Cabrol. "Mozarabe (La Liturgie)." In

Dictionnaire d'Archéologie Chrétienne et de Liturgie, edited by Fernand Cabrol and Henri Leclercq, vol. 2-A. Paris: Librairie Letouzey et Ané, 1935.

Mancini, Guido. *San Isidoro de Sevilla: Aspectos Literarios.* Publicaciones del Instituto Caro y Cuervo, Series Minor 4. Bogotá, 1955.

Muldowney, Mary Sarah, trans. *Saint Augustine: Treatises on Various Subjects.* Fathers of the Church 16. Washington, DC: Catholic University of America Press, 1952.

The New American Bible. Sponsored by The Bishops' Committee of the Confraternity of Christian Doctrine. Camden, NJ: Thomas Nelson Inc., 1971.

O'Callaghan, Joseph F. *A History of Medieval Spain.* Ithaca, NY/London: Cornell University Press, 1975. Reprint, Cornell Paperbacks, 1994.

Pelikan, Jaroslav. *The Growth of Medieval Theology (600–1300).* Volume 3, *The Christian Tradition: A History of the Development of Doctrine.* Chicago: University of Chicago Press, 1978.

Pérez de Urbel, Fray Justo. *San Isidoro de Sevilla: Su Vida, Su Obra y Su Tiempo.* 3rd ed. León: Universidad de León, 1995.

Pinell, Jordi, OSB [J. M. Pinell or Jorge M. Pinell]. *Liturgia hispánica.* Edited by José Aldazábal. Biblioteca Litúrgica 9. Barcelona: Centre de Pastoral Litúrgica, 1998.

──────. "Missale Hispano-Mozarabicum." *Notitiæ* 24 (1988): 670–727.

──────. "El problema de las dos tradiciones del antiguo rito hispánico. Valoración documental de la tradición B, en vistas a una eventual revisión del Ordinario de la Misa Mozárabe." In *Liturgia y Música Mozárabes: Ponencias y Comunicaciones presentadas al I Congreso Internacional de Estudios Mozárabes: Toledo, 1975,* 3–44, Serie D, no. 1. Toledo: Instituto de Estudios Visigóticos-Mozárabes de San Eugenio, 1978.

──────. "Los textos de la antigua liturgia hispánica: Fuentes para su estudio." *Estudios sobre la liturgia mozárabe.* [Toledo] (1965): 109–64.

La Provincia de Andalucía SJ, ed. *Miscellanea Isidoriana. Homenaje a S. Isidoro de Sevilla en el XIII Centenario de su Muerte 636–4 de Abril–1936.* Rome: Gregorian University Press, 1936.

Rivera Recio, Juan Francisco. "La iglesia mozárabe." In *Historia de la Iglesia en España,* vol. 2, pt. 1, *La iglesia de los siglos VIII al XIV,* 22–60. Biblioteca de Autores Cristianos 17. Madrid: Edica, 1982.

Roman Missal. Revised by decree of the Second Vatican Council and Published by Authority of Pope Paul VI: *The Sacramentary,* approved for use in the Dioceses of the United States of America by the National Conference of Catholic Bishops and Confirmed by the Apostolic See. Eng. trans. prep. by ICEL. New York: Catholic Book Pub. Co., 1985.

Sotomayor y Muro, Manuel. "La Iglesia hispana en la época de transición." In *Historia de la Iglesia en España,* vol. 1, *La Iglesia en la España romana y visigoda*, 372–400. Biblioteca de Autores Christianos 16. Madrid: Edica, 1979.

———. "Sobre los orígenes del cristianismo en Hispania." In *Historia de la Iglesia en España*, vol. 1. 1:120–65.

Stocking, Rachel L. *Bishops, Councils, and Consensus in the Visigothic Kingdom, 589–633*. Ann Arbor, MI: University of Michigan Press, 2000.

Val, U. D. del. "Isidoro de Sevilla." *Diccionario de Historia Eclesiástica de España*, dirigido por Quintín Aldea Vaquero, Tomás Marín Martínez, José Vives Gatell, vol. 2, Madrid: Instituto Enrique Flórez, 1972.

Vicens Vives, Jaime. *Approaches to the History of Spain*. 2nd rev. ed. Translated and edited by Joan Connelly Ullman. Berkeley: University of California Press, 1970. First published 1967; original published in Spanish as *Aproximación a la historia de España* (Barcelona: Editorial Vicens-Vives, 1952); English translation based on the 2nd edition published by Editorial Teide, 1960, for the Centro de Estudios Históricos Internacionales, Universidad de Barcelona.

Vinayo González, Antonio. *San Isidoro de Sevilla: Su Doctrina y Su Pensamiento en 500 Aforismos y Sentencias*. León: Editorial Isidoriana, 2000.

Vives, José, Tomás Marín Martínez, and Gonzalo Martínez Díez, eds. *Concilios Visigóticas e Hispano-Romanos*. Barcelona/Madrid: Consejo Superior de Investigaciones Científicas Instituto Enrizue Florez, 1963.

Vogel, Cyrille. *Medieval Liturgy: An Introduction to the Sources*. Revised and translated by William G. Storey and Niels Krogh Rasmussen, OP, with the assistance of John K. Brooks-Leonard. Washington, DC: Pastoral Press, 1986; revised and updated from *Introduction aux sources de l'histoire du culte chrétien au moyen age*, 1981.

Walker, Rose. *Views of Transition: Liturgy and Illumination in Medieval Spain*. British Library Studies in Medieval Culture. Toronto/Buffalo: University of Toronto Press, 1998; first published, London: British Library, 1998.

Wegman, Herman. *Christian Worship in East and West: A Study Guide to Liturgical History*. Translated by Gordon W. Lathrop. Collegeville, MN: A Pueblo Book, Liturgical Press, 1985, 1990. Original Dutch publication, *Geschiedenis van de Christelijke Eredienst in het Westen en in het Oosten* (Hilversum: Gooi en Sticht bv, 1976).

Witczak, Michael. "The Sacramentary of Paul VI." In *The Eucharist*, vol. 3, *Handbook for Liturgical Studies*. Edited by Anscar J. Chupungco, 3:133–75. Collegeville, MN: A Pueblo Book, Liturgical Press, 1999.

INDEX